The

The complete Jade Russell

The
Complete Jack Russell
James McKay

Quiller

First published in the UK in 2000
by Swan Hill Press, an imprint of Quiller Publishing Ltd
Reprinted 2002, 2006
Reprinted under the Quiller imprint 2009

British Library Cataloguing-in-Publication Data
A catalogue record for this book
is available from the British Library

ISBN 978 1 84037 119 2

Typeset by Phoenix Typesetting, Auldgirth, Dumfriesshire
Printed in Malta by Gutenberg Press Ltd

Quiller

An imprint of Quiller Publishing Ltd
Wykey House, Wykey, Shrewsbury, SY4 1JA
Tel: 01939 261616 Fax: 01939 261606
E-mail: info@quillerbooks.com
Website: www.countrybooksdirect.com

DEDICATION

This book is dedicated, unreservedly, to my wife Jane, and my son, Thomas, without whom it would never have appeared.

CONTENTS

INTRODUCTION

Jack Russell terriers – known to thousands simply as JRs or Jacks – hold a special place in the heart of many country people, not least because of the work that such terriers carry out in the British countryside. Many farmers would be lost without their Jack Russells to catch mice and rats, help with the hunting of rabbits, and assist with the tracking down and culling of those foxes intent on killing the farmer's chickens, ducks or sheep.

I well remember my rabbiting trips, aided by my ferrets and my first Jack Russell terrier. The JR – 'Britt' – would let me know which of the many holes in the ground really were rabbit burrows and which, if any, actually contained any rabbits. She would bound along, sniffing at every little indentation in the land, sticking her nose as far as she could down any tunnels she found, and all the time her excitement was plain for all to see. When she found a hole with a rabbit at home, she would bound back to me, jump high in the air in front of me – as only JRs seem to do – and then go bounding back to the hole to take another sniff. She would keep this up for as long as it took me to start getting out my purse nets, at which time she would walk tightly alongside me, almost as if she were tied to my left ankle by a 15 cm piece of cord. All this time, she would be very quiet, although her tail – right the way down to past her backside – would never be still. As I entered my ferrets and retired away from the holes, Britt would be with me, but walking backwards, eager to ensure that she missed none of the action.

As the rabbits began to bolt, Britt would rush to any that were caught in a purse net – action that ensured that I did not miss any. If a rabbit should slip the net, Britt was hard on its heels and, in cover, almost always caught the rabbit, killing it with a quick shake of her head, and then brought the dead rabbit to me. It was a very sad day in the McKay household when Britt passed on.

I admire Jack Russell terriers, in a way in which I admire very few other animals. They are hard working, they make great pets and superb house dogs. Although they obviously lack the physical stature of a breed such as a German shepherd dog, they more than make up for this with their willingness to protect their pack members and their territory. They are the bravest little dogs I have

1

ever known, and will always give any householder ample warning of any incursions onto the family territory by any unauthorised people. What more could one ask for in a small pet dog?

Recently, one particular breed of Jack Russell has been recognised by the Kennel Club, the governing body of dog breeding in the United Kingdom. This has been a controversial move, with the JR world split asunder into two distinct camps. One, the Jack Russell Terrier Club of Great Britain (JRTCGB) will have nothing to do with the Kennel Club, not least because the club believes that the standard adopted by the Kennel Club is wrong, and not what the 'Sporting Parson' (Parson John Russell, the originator of the breed which even today bears his name) intended. The other faction is the Parson Jack Russell Club, which made the moves which resulted in the recognition by the Kennel Club of the 'Parson Jack Russell terrier'.

I will not take sides on this issue, but merely record the facts of what has actually happened. Above all, though, I sincerely hope that the real Jack Russell terrier goes from strength to strength and that, eventually, all factions can reach some middle ground. For that is what we are famous for in Great Britain – our sense of reason and compromise.

In this book, I have sought to give full instructions and guidance to those who wish to keep and/or breed a Jack Russell terrier. I have deliberately avoided going into any detail concerning the working of this brave little terrier, even though that is what the Sporting Parson bred the dog for. I feel that that is too specialised an area for a book such as this. However, the reader should not take this as any kind of disapproval of working Jack Russell terriers; far from it. Country sports are an integral and vital part of the British countryside. If any of the established country sports should disappear, the British countryside, and all of Great Britain will be a sadder, weaker and less British place, and I – along with countless millions of others – hope such a day will never come.

If you wish to find out more about working your Jack Russell terrier – for that was the intention of the Parson when he started this wonderful breed – then you should contact a good club, or the Countryside Alliance, who will do all they can to help you in your endeavours to hunt legitimate quarry with your terrier.

I have been helped in the production of this book by many people. In particular Brian Male, and received encouragement and guidance from many others. I thank them for their help and patience, and would point out that any mistakes that occur in this book are mine and mine alone.

In particular, I would like to thank my wife, Jane, and my son, Thomas. Between them, Jane and Thomas have helped immeasurably, and have always given me encouragement by words and deeds. I am sure that, were it not for the countless cups of coffee brought to me by my wife, and the hard work of both my wife and son put into keeping the McKay household and menagerie ticking along, this book would never have been written. Thank you both, I owe you a great deal.

To all Jack Russell terrier enthusiasts, I hope you enjoy this book, and I hope to see more of you over the coming years, at country fairs, shows and in the field.

JAMES McKAY
Derbyshire

CHAPTER 1

THE BEGINNING

History of the breed

The Jack Russell terrier has a long and well documented history, since it was established in the early 19th Century by the Reverend John Russell of Devon, England, who was an avid fox hunter. But terriers of different sorts were around much earlier, and it is from these that Russell developed the terrier which bears his name today.

Vicar of Swimbridge, Devon, England, John Russell was born on 21 December 1795, from a family established in Devon since 1549. In that year, Lord John Russell had been sent to the West Country to quell and suppress the prayer-book riots, and the family remained in the area.

John Russell's father, a curate, was a very keen fox-hunting man, and was often missing from his church duties on hunting days. It was even said that it was not unusual to see the curate, conducting his church duties, with the tops of his hunting boots showing under his cassock. To help make ends meet, Mr Russell taught private lessons, and often rewarded his charges with a day's hunting.

John junior was sent to school at Blundell's in Tiverton, one of England's great public schools of the time. Life at Blundell's was tough; breakfast was one bread roll and a cup of watered-down milk, meat served to the boys was often 'high', and the forks had only one prong. The headmaster of the day, Dr William Richards, was firmly of the belief that the only way to teach young boys was to knock it into them, and he often began the school day by flogging one of the boys, often for a very trivial misdemeanour.

The school was so cold in the winter that the ink in the ink wells was regularly frozen and, as there were no bathrooms at the school, John Russell and his fellow pupils had to carry out their morning ablutions under a pump in the school yard.

While at Blundell's, Russell junior, like many of his contemporaries, was subjected to bullying. Russell, however, decided to get revenge on at least one of his tormentors, a monitor by the name of Hunter.

Dr Richards heard that many of the boys were illicitly keeping pet rabbits at the school, which was strictly against the school rules. Dr Richards ordered that all rabbits must be disposed of immediately, but Hunter sought to hide his. Russell, however, had other ideas, and took his ferrets to the place were Hunter's pet rabbits were kept. There, Russell placed a ferret in each of the rabbit hutches, with obvious results. Unfortunately for Russell, Hunter reported the matter to the headmaster, who duly flogged young Russell.

The headmaster also made Russell get rid of his ferrets, and this led Russell to carry out illicit ferreting forays on local farms, using ferrets he kept outside the school. He made friends with the farmers on whose land he ferreted, and between them, Russell, a school friend, and the farmers came up with the idea of keeping hounds to give them all sport.

Within a short time, Russell and his friends had acquired four and a half couple (nine) of hounds, which local hunts had pensioned off. These hounds were kennelled with a friendly blacksmith who lived close to the school. The farmers ensured that the hounds were kept supplied with adequate amounts of flesh to feed them, and all was well. But things could not last, and Russell was reported to the headmaster by a sneak who signed his letter 'Friend of Good Discipline'. The outcome of the disclosure was that Russell was almost expelled from Blundell's.

Obviously spurred on by this near disaster, Russell put his nose to the grindstone and worked so hard that he won an award and a medal for elocution. Russell used part of his winnings to buy his first horse, from the Reverend John Froude, who swindled the young man in the deal.

While out hunting one day, Russell lost some of his hounds and had a chance encounter which led him to experience his first day's stag hunting. While searching for the hounds, Russell met Dr William Palk Collyns, the author of the first and arguably one of the best books on stag hunting. Under Palk Collyns' direction, Russell managed to be in at the kill, near Slade Bridge. This event changed his life and he hunted with the stag hounds for nearly seventy years.

Russell went on to Exeter College, Oxford, a college that was noted for classics. However, Russell soon learned that very few of his fellow undergraduates were interested in academic studies at all. Almost all the students were the sons of country squires and gentlemen, and as such their main interests were undoubtedly hunting, shooting and fishing. So long as lectures and, of course, chapel, were attended fairly regularly by the students, there was very little, if any, interference from the lecturing staff. Russell took full advantage of this wonderful state of affairs, and hunted regularly with the Beaufort, the Bicester, and the Old Berkshire. His only constraint was his lack of funds. Rather than admit to his financial problems, Russell would make excuses about his health when invited hunting, but there can be little doubt that, if he could have afforded it, Russell would have been out hunting on every possible occasion, and his studies would have suffered. Russell went on to successfully complete his finals, and got his degree.

Whilst out hunting, Russell carefully observed the methods and tactics employed by the huntsmen, in particular Payne and Goodall, huntsmen of the Beaufort and the Bicester, respectively. Both of these men were in the very top echelons of professional huntsmen, and Russell was to later make great use of the lessons learned by hunting with and observing these men.

In 1820, Russell became a priest, just one year after being ordained as a deacon. He became curate of George Nympton, near South Molton, a position that Russell soon realised took up very little of his time, even when he took up the duties in nearby South Molton in addition to his own parish. He decided to make good use of this spare time, and got together five couple of hounds, which he kennelled with various friends in the parish. Russell attempted to hunt otters with this pack, but neither he nor his hounds had any experience of hunting such a quarry, and despite his thorough working of all the riversides of Exmoor, not one otter was found by the pack.

Russell being the man he was, however, did not consider the efforts to be a waste of time, as he came to know the area better than most men, and he would use this intimate knowledge to his advantage in later years.

By chance, Russell met a local farmer who had a hound for sale, and Russell jumped at the opportunity to add experience to his little pack. The new hound, Racer, was experienced at hunting, and had actually hunted otters before. Racer quickly led Russell's pack to success, and the pack killed 35 otters in a very short time. Russell hunted these 'otter hounds' during the summer season, for over six years, while hunting fox with the Revd John Froude's pack in the winter. At this time, Russell also became friendly with George Templer, Master of a pack of dwarf foxhounds in Stover. Templer used to keep caged and chained foxes, which were let out – in full view of the hounds – to be hunted. On almost every occasion, the fox was recovered without any injury, due to the absolute control which Templer had over his pack. Russell learned a lot from Templer.

On 30 May 1826, Russell married Miss Penelope Incledon Bury, the daughter of Admiral and Mrs Bury of Dennington (near Barnstaple, Devon), and shortly afterwards, moved to become curate to his father, at Iddesleigh, near Hatherleigh. The Russell's first child – a son – died as an infant, and a second son – Bury – was born a short time afterwards.

It wasn't long before Russell again gave thought and action to his main love – hunting. He acquired a pack of about twelve couple, mainly from the Stover pack, which had been broken up after the death of George Templer. As there were local hunts very close to him, Russell did not enjoy a large country over which to hunt, but persuaded the nearest two Masters – the Revd Peter Glubb,

A fine brace of working JRs await their turn at a dig.

of Torrington, and the Hon. Newton Fellowes of Eggesford – to give him permission to draw coverts on the periphery of their countries.

However, as the local villagers killed foxes on sight, caring nothing about the sport of fox hunting, Russell was faced with such a scarcity of foxes that he also had to hunt hares and polecats. Within a couple of years, Russell had persuaded the locals not to kill foxes, but to leave them for his sport, and he also earned the respect of the locals by his actions and hunting prowess. In fact, such was Russell's success, that it wasn't long before many local landowners were asking him to hunt over their land. In 1828, Russell's pack had found 32 foxes, and accounted for 28 of them. In addition, the pack had taken 146 hares (these had been hunted on those days when no foxes could be found in Russell's hunting country).

All of this hunting, of course, cost money, and as no subscriptions were ever asked of those who rode with Russell's hounds, Russell himself had to stand the not inconsiderable expense of his pack. This caused a great strain on Russell's finances, and so, while retaining the ownership of his hounds, Russell merged his pack with Mr C.A. Harris of Hayne, who shared the expenses of the merged pack, now numbering over seventy couple; however this number was soon reduced to thirty-five couple.

Russell's affable nature and his hunting prowess earned him many friends and accolades, and he was soon hunting far from home, with his hunting country growing almost daily; it soon extended from Torrington to Bodmin, a distance of almost seventy miles. By Russell's third year at Iddlesleigh, Russell's country had become too big to be tenable, and many foxes were causing a great deal of damage on some estates within Russell's country. Consequently, another pack – under Tom Phillips – was started and took over much of Russell's country. This caused much bad feeling and animosity, and this would have gone from bad to worse had it not been that, in 1832, Russell was offered – and accepted – the perpetual curacy of Swymbridge and Landkey, near Barnstaple, Devon.

At Swymbridge, John and Penelope Russell lived in a house called Tordown, which stands high above the village, and were both given a great welcome because of Penelope's having been born and bred at nearby Dennington House, and so she was considered to be a native, and John's fame in the hunting field. Swymbridge (now Swimbridge) has very little of outstanding beauty or interest, except perhaps for the church and a pub, now called 'The Jack Russell', but which, in Russell's time, was known as 'The New Inn'. The sign of the pub is a replica of a painting of Russell's first terrier, 'Trump', both indications of the importance placed on the village's connection with Parson Jack Russell, and the terriers named after him.

Before leaving Iddesleigh, Russell had disbanded his pack, and now firmly ensconced at Swymbridge, he set about building a new pack of hounds. His first acquisitions consisted of six-and-a-half couple from the Vine Hunt but, not long after their arrival, several of his parishioners told Russell that it would be 'unseemly' for the vicar to keep hounds, and so he prepared to send them back to his old pack. It was only the intervention of his wife that persuaded Russell to ignore the sentiments expressed by some of his parishioners, and keep the hounds. He seems to have done a great job at ignoring these sentiments, as he remained as Master of Hounds until 1871.

Russell's new bishop was Henry Philpotts, a man who severely disapproved of clergy hunting and, although Russell made a fine first impression on the bishop, it was not too long before he crossed swords with his new boss. Russell was accused of failing to bury a dead child on the day on which the child's parents wished, because it was a hunting day. When questioned by the bishop, the child's mother said that the charge was untrue, a fact which severely upset the bishop, who was intent on finding some reason for reprimanding Russell. After trying – totally unsuccessfully – to find charges on which Russell could be successfully prosecuted, the bishop informed Russell that he (Russell) must give up his hounds and hunting; Russell refused. As Russell had not broken an ecclesiastical law, he could not be sacked from his job, but the bishop spitefully threatened to sack Russell's curate. Only a petition from the parishioners saved the curate's job, which he held until his marriage.

Penelope Russell died in 1875, and Russell took the loss very badly. He threw himself into his work in an effort to help him overcome his grief, preaching for many charities and suchlike. Despite this, he was lonely until his death; his son, Bury, was always in severe financial difficulties, even being declared bankrupt on one occasion. Bury, however, eventually managed to turn himself around, and became a bank manager in Barnstaple.

In 1879, Russell was offered the living at Black Torrington, at more than double his current salary, and his financial position forced him to accept, although he was extremely unhappy about the move. The parishioners of Swymbridge held a testimonial for Russell, to which the Prince of Wales contributed, and the esteem in which this gallant old preacher was held can be witnessed by the fact that the testimonial raised almost £800. With this, the parishioners bought Russell a silver soup tureen and gave him a cheque for the remaining money.

When he arrived at Black Torrington, Russell discovered that his fame had preceded him. He was given a great welcome in his new parish, with all the local bells ringing out for him. While waiting for his house to be completed, Russell stayed with a local notable and was happy with his new environment, but soon realised how unhappy he was about missing Exmoor. To get over this, Russell raised a new pack (of eight couple of harriers). Suffering from ill health and sensing his end was close, Russell eventually parted with this pack and presented the hounds to Henry Villebois.

John Russell died on 28 April 1883 in Bude, at the age of 88.

Russell's terriers

Russell needed a dog with spirit and endurance to help with his favourite sport. As mentioned earlier, Russell's first terrier was a bitch called Trump, which he acquired on a May afternoon towards the end of his time at Oxford. Russell was walking towards Marston when he met a milkman on his rounds. The milkman (whose name history has not seen fit to record) had with him a terrier with which Russell was immediately smitten, and Russell bought the dog on the spot. Trump was to become the progenitress of the terrier which still bears the Parson's name today – the Jack Russell terrier.

Trump was pure white, except for a patch of dark tan over each eye, and another 'not larger than a penny piece' at the root of the tail. The coat was rather wiry, and the overall size was said to be very similar to that of an adult vixen fox.

Although a founder member of the UK's Kennel Club, Russell, along with many other hunting and shooting men of his day, was extremely suspicious of the dogs seen in the show ring. Russell knew what he wanted in a hunting dog – gameness – and the 'aesthetic perfection' of the show dogs did not impress him one iota. These feelings were compounded by the fact that, because of their monetary value, none of these show dogs were ever given the opportunity to prove themselves – or otherwise – at the job for which fox terriers had always been bred – working foxes. Russell also went against the fashion of his time, by not having any of his terriers' tails docked, nor their ears cut.

Legend has it that all of the Parson's line of terriers were the result of matings from dogs and bitches from within the West Country, but there is evidence to show that, on at least one occasion, Russell brought in an outcross from outside the West Country. Some of the progenitors of Russell's line of terriers were Old Jock, Old Tartar, Old Trap and Grove Nettle.

Jock was pupped in 1859, bred by Jack Morgan, whipper-in to the Grove Hunt. Tartar was a tough-looking dog who beat Jock on the show bench on at least two occasions. Jock weighed about 8 kilos, had a black patch on his stern and a dun patch on one ear. Tartar weighed slightly less and was pure white except for a pale tan patch over one eye. Tartar's breeding is not known, and when he was shown at the Birmingham show in 1863, he was described as 'pedigreeless'.

Russell kept his line going by carefully selecting and breeding his terriers, using other dogs which seemed to have the abilities for which he was looking.

Only the Parson Jack Russell terrier is recognised by the UK's Kennel Club.

The Jack Russell Terrier Club of Great Britain have their own standard.

He kept detailed and accurate records of all of his terrier breeding activities, and selected for temperament, courage and conformation (type) equally.

Although today many owners work their Jack Russell terriers on rabbits, rats and other animals, Russell would never choose to work his terriers on any animal other than a fox, and the terriers regularly followed hounds for 15–20 miles at a time. It was not the practice, in Russell's time, for the hunt to use a terrier man, but rather for the terriers to run behind the hounds, following the trail if they got left behind or could not keep up the pace. This caused problems since there were many badger setts around Russell's hunting country – in fact too many for them all to be stopped. Consequently it was far from an unusual occurrence for foxes to go to earth in a badger sett. As many of these setts were huge, it was impractical to dig out such foxes but, as the terriers were left very much to their own devices, it was often impossible to prevent terriers going into the sett and to ground. Also, it was not the practice for the hunt to carry their own digging implements and so, if the terriers went to ground a distance from the nearest village or farm from whence suitable digging equipment could be procured or borrowed, extracting the terriers and fox was nigh on impossible.

In order to try to prevent foxes going to ground, Russell perfected a recipe for a concoction which would be sprinkled around the mouth of the earth or sett. It smelled so foul that, if any were spilled on the hands or clothing of the man assigned to sprinkle the mixture, that person would be made less than welcome by his fellows for many days, as no amount of scrubbing and washing could shift the smell.

With today's hunts utilising the services of terrier men, terriers are not allowed to go to ground in unsuitable areas, and so these problems rarely – if ever – exist today.

While many JR adherents will argue that Russell created a separate breed of terriers, historical fact does not support this. What Russell bred was a type of terrier – in fact a type which totally conformed to the Kennel Club standard of the time. The big difference between Russell and many of his contemporaries was that Russell wanted to – and did – prove the gameness of his terriers, and I feel quite confident that, such was the Parson's strict adherence to his own high standards and criteria, any terrier that did not meet those exacting standards was never bred from by Russell, and that most – if not all – of these 'failures' were put down very quickly.

Post-Russell breeding

The next name to be associated with the Jack Russell terrier is that of Arthur Blake Heinemann, a man born in Sussex in 1871, but who lived most of his life on Exmoor.

Affection shared between a JR and its owner. Such bonds are the main reason why many people wish to keep dogs, and the JR is understandably one of the more popular breeds for those living in towns and cities . . .

Heinemann obtained his original terrier stock from Squire Nicholas Snow, of Oare; Snow had obtained his original stock from John Russell. Heinemann was helped in his endeavours by his kennel maid Annie Rawle, who was related to John Russell's kennelman, Will Rawle, and their combined knowledge helped in the management and breeding of Heinemann's terriers. Annie was in sole control of Heinemann's kennels during the First World War (1914–1918), when Heinemann was serving his country, and again on the death of Heinemann.

Heinemann was a great badger digger (a legal pastime then), and founded the Devon & Somerset Badger Club in 1894; part of that club's raison d'être, along with promoting badger digging, was the breeding of good working

. . . as well as for country-dwellers.

terriers. Later, the club's name was changed to The Parson Jack Russell Club.

Heinemann was like John Russell, in that he insisted that gameness was the premier requisite of any terrier. Like Russell, he also kept detailed records and pedigrees of his dogs, and on his death, these passed to Annie Rawle, now married and known as Annie Harris. She took these to the West Country author, Henry Williamson, in the hope that they could be used in a biography. They never were, and it is not known what happened to this paperwork.

Heinemann insisted on breeding true to Russell's blood line and created superb kennels of terriers. He was also something of a sporting journalist, a fact which saved his bacon in later life. He was not money-wise, and lost most of what he earned, having to scale down his living accordingly. He was saved from complete destitution by the editor of *The Shooting Times*, Tim Sedgewick, who appointed Heinemann as hunting editor for the weekly newspaper.

Heinemann died as a result of a day's coursing. On New Year's Day 1930, a bitterly cold day, while out coursing, he fell into a pond, but despite his sixty years, refused to go home to change out of his wet clothes until the end of the coursing day. Not surprisingly, Heinemann contracted pneumonia, and died within a week.

Another name forever linked with the Jack Russell is that of Alys Serrell, author of the book *With Hound and Terrier in the Field*. Alys' founder dog was named Redcap, born in 1890 and of unknown ancestory, and was smooth-coated. He had a white coat, with a bright tan-coloured head and a black mark under his right ear; he weighed about seven kilos. He was mated to Amber, a bitch by a grandson of Russell's dog Tip. Later, Alys' terrier became the foundation of another famous Jack Russell terrier kennel, that of Miss Augusta Guest.

Many of today's Jack Russell terriers can be traced back to some of the kennels and dogs listed in this chapter.

Today's Jack Russell terrier

Unfortunately, today one can be very misled by adverts offering 'Jack Russell terriers', as almost any terrier type of dog (particularly if they have a predominance of white in their coat) is erroneously referred to as a Jack Russell terrier. Further confusion is created by the fact that the British Kennel Club now recognises a form of Jack Russell terrier, the Parson Jack Russell terrier. This recognition was achieved by the Parson Jack Russell Terrier Club on their second attempt in 1989, and the official recognition of the breed was given in March 1990, via an announcement in the Kennel Club's own publication, the *Kennel Gazette*. While the adherents of the PJRT will no doubt claim that theirs is THE Jack Russell terrier, others would dispute that claim, not least of all the members of the Jack Russell Terrier Club of Great Britain.

However, the aim of this book is not to support any of the sides in that argument, merely to ensure that those of us who really appreciate the many benefits of this intelligent, enthusiastic, loyal, excitable canine can care for our charges throughout their lives.

The true Jack Russell terrier has predominantly white colouring with a combination of black and tan markings with a strong body style. The coat varies in length, but the dog should have a short tail, carried high, along with a flat wide head with a slightly pointed muzzle. Black nose and lips, small v-shaped ears that fall forward and almond-shaped, deep-set dark brown eyes show the character of this game little dog, and its short legs and muscular thighs clearly illustrate the dog's hunting ancestry.

Above all, a true Jack Russell is a dog with oodles of charisma, style and character!

CHAPTER 2

SELECTION

Whether you intend to show your JR, want to establish your own line or merely want a pet, the selection of a puppy should be given much thought. No one should ever buy any animal on impulse, as this will only end in an unsatisfactory purchase, and unhappy times for both dog and humans involved.

Much caution should be observed before rushing in to buy a JR. While some will see the dog's tenacity, others will see its bloody-mindedness, some will see its boundless energy and enthusiasm while others will see a dog which just has to have action. In other words one person's idea of a pleasing and wanted characteristic may easily be another's idea of an extremely serious drawback. One man's meat is another man's poison; not everyone will suit a dog, and even fewer will suit a JR.

Once you have decided that you really want a JR – and this decision should involve all the family, as all will be, to a greater or lesser degree, affected by the decision – you must give more thought to the detail of what you want, and where you will be able to get it.

What to look for

Firstly, the potential purchaser should decide the reason for wanting a JR. If the sole or main purpose is to show the dog in Kennel Club approved shows, perhaps with the ambition of a win at Cruft's, the dog must conform to the Kennel Club standards for the Parson Jack Russell terrier. If you wish to show your JR in shows organised by the Jack Russell Club of Great Britain, you will find that a different breed standard exists, and so your JR must be chosen with this in mind.

Even if you intend to work your JR, or simply keep it as a household pet, much thought should be given to its selection. Beauty may well be in the eye of the beholder, but a JR should always look like a JR.

Many people still like to see a JR with a coloured head.

Whatever your reasons for choosing a JR, the following should be borne in mind before final selection of the individual JR is made:

Where will you purchase your JR?
What should you look for to indicate a sound, healthy terrier?
What should you avoid in your purchase?
Which sex?
How do you assess the character of your intended purchases?
At what age should your JR be obtained?

Let us examine all of these questions.

Where to purchase your JR

JRs are sold by many people, from the person who lovingly cares for his terriers, and simply breeds one or two litters to ensure continuation of his line, to commercial breeders who breed from their terriers in order to make money. In between these two extremes are many others, who include good and bad JR keepers, all with their reasons for breeding and selling the animals.

Wherever possible, go to an established breeder who has a proven

Young children love all dogs, even those used for hunting purposes, like these hounds.

reputation, and who has been keeping and breeding and, if you intend to show your JR, winning at shows for several years. While no such person will let you have their very best JR – they will want to keep those for their own purposes – neither will they risk a hard-earned reputation by selling you inferior stock.

When buying, try to visit the breeder's home or base of operations, and look carefully at the parents of the JRs being offered for sale, along with all other animals kept by the seller. All kennels should be clean, of an adequate size, and not overcrowded.

Are the dogs all in good condition? What are they being fed on? Some breeders will try to cut corners to save themselves time, trouble and, of course, money, and will feed inadequate diets, and so the offspring of these malnourished animals may well be suffering because of this. It is the future owners who will reap the rewards of this poor treatment, and have large vet fees or deformed and useless terriers to deal with.

A healthy puppy will have loose skin, which will pick up easily, rather than stick to the terrier's bones, and it will be pleasantly plump, but not have a distended stomach. The puppy should be free from all external parasites, and this includes any mites in the ears, which should be examined thoroughly. The owner of the pups should also be scrutinised, and you should expect that to be reciprocated, as none of us want 'our' puppies to go to the wrong home.

It is also important to ascertain what criteria the JRs have been bred to, as owners will have differing ideas as to what makes a good JR.

There are commercial breeders and dealers and even, unfortunately, 'puppy farms' which exist merely to mass produce puppies for the market-place. While many commercial breeders will do everything to ensure that the puppies they produce are fit, healthy and happy, and will often take steps to provide the puppies with good caring homes by careful selection of potential buyers; puppy farms will not. These places are there merely to ensure that the owners make money, even if it is at the expense of the puppies or their parents. Very often, pressure is put on visitors to these establishments to buy a puppy, even though that breed or that individual puppy will not be suitable for the humans concerned. I would never dream of visiting such an establishment, let alone buying a dog from one, and I would urge readers to treat these places in the same manner.

By giving consideration, time and effort to the choice of the supplier of your JR, you will reap the benefits. It really is worth the effort, even if this also involves a waiting period. As your dog could be with you for fifteen or so years, you will have time to rue your impatience and lack of thought.

What to look for and what to avoid

A healthy JR will have loads of energy and a *joie de vivre*, bouncing around in his kennel, and playing with his siblings or kennel mates. His eyes will be

Some JRs have very little coloration, being almost entirely white.

bright, ears held erect, coat shiny and clean, and his motions will be solid.

An ill terrier will be entirely different; he will be lethargic, lying down and sleeping for much of the day. His ears will be flat against his head, his coat matted, dirty, staring and greasy to the touch; he may have a discharge from his eyes, ears, sex opening or anus, and he may also have diarrhoea.

Under no circumstances should you buy any terrier from a kennel containing one or more animals as described in the last paragraph; to do so would be foolish, since even if the terrier which you purchase is not exhibiting the symptoms, he is almost certain to be infected and, if you place him with others, he will pass on this ailment to all the dogs with which he comes into contact.

There are also physical deformities that you should be aware of, and naturally avoid. I list them in alphabetical order.

Achondroplasia (Dwarfism)

The result of this inherited problem is to produce very small JRs, the size (or rather lack thereof) being most obvious in the very short, stumpy legs of the

A young JR which exemplifies the musculature so necessary for the terrier to carry out a full day's work.

animals. All too common a defect in some areas, and puppies showing such deformity should be avoided at all costs, and NEVER bred from.

Bones

If a puppy has not received top class nutrition while in the womb and in its early life, it will not grow into a fit and healthy dog which is capable of carrying out a full day's work. A lack of calcium in the diet of the pregnant bitch and consequently in the nursing bitch and her litter, will inevitably result in poor bone formation. 'Bow legs' may also result from a genetic defect, and so all animals showing abnormalities of the legs should be treated with great suspicion and, if at all possible, totally avoided. Obviously any animal exhibiting any defect or abnormality which may be genetic must not be used for breeding purposes.

Cryptorchidism

In normal male JRs, both testes can be seen when the dog is a few weeks old. If this is not the case, then there could be a potentially serious problem, particularly if it is intended to breed or show the JR in question. Monorchids have one testicle that has descended, with the other hidden, while cryptorchids have no testicles descended. The term cryptorchid actually literally translates to 'hidden testicle', and so the lack of one or both testes must be investigated. If the dog in question has had both testes removed surgically, he should be referred to as a castrate.

The causes of cryptorchidism could include the testicle(s) being hidden in the abdomen, or in the passage through the various layers of the abdominal muscles. They may even be outside the muscles, but under the skin; if this is the case, they can be easily located by feeling the area carefully.

As almost every cryptorchid causes problems, the dog would be severely penalised or even disqualified in the show ring (depending on the rules pertaining) and is almost invariably sterile (or at the very least has an extremely low sperm count), I strongly recommend that, unless your dog is destined only to be a pet, or you have already decided to have him castrated, such animals should be avoided. Those who purchase such animals are strongly advised to have them surgically castrated at an early age.

Dew claws

Puppies are born with dew claws (the vestigial remains of a fifth toe). Some pups have them only on their forelegs, while others also have them on their hindlegs. If left intact, they can be a cause of trouble in later life, particularly for working JRs, and so are almost routinely removed by an experienced person or a veterinary surgeon. The operation is usually carried out while the pups are very young, and before their eyes have opened. By doing this, there is no legal or other necessity to administer any anaesthetic. In some countries, such operations may only be carried out by qualified veterinary surgeons, but even in those areas where lay people are allowed to conduct such operations, expert and experienced guidance should be sought. All instruments used must be sterilised before and after each pup, to limit the risk of cross-infection. Ensure that the dam is out of ear-shot before commencing this operation.

Hernia

A soft swelling in the region of the umbilicus may well indicate a hernia (known as an umbilical hernia, for obvious reasons), and although minor hernias in young pups can often heal themselves, more serious ones will require surgery, with all of its incumbent risks. If in any doubt, avoid such puppies.

Jaw

There are two major possible faults with a JR's jaw; the jaw may be under-shot or overshot. In undershot animals, the lower jaw protrudes beyond the upper one, while the opposite is true in the case of overshot JRs, i.e. the upper jaw protrudes beyond the lower one. There is strong evidence to suggest that this fault is inherited, and such dogs must never be bred from, even if the deformity appears to be only slight. Such deformities will inevitably be penalised in the show ring, and may well adversely affect the career of a working JR. Obviously such animals are best avoided.

Tail

As in many animals, a JR's tail can show deformation at birth. As the tail is merely an extension of the spine, a kink in the tail may well indicate serious potential problems, and would be penalised in the show ring. Again, such animals should not be bred from.

Another point regarding the tail is its length. While John Russell's original bitch had a docked tail, in line with contemporary fashion, Russell himself is said not to have indulged in this practice, but to have selectively bred his terriers for short tails. In the UK, since 1993 it has been illegal for lay persons to carry out the surgical removal of the tail or part of the tail, i.e. docking. This was made so by an amendment to the Veterinary Surgeons Act, following a long campaign by some animal welfare groups and the Royal College of Veterinary Surgeons.

To exacerbate the problems for those who wish to have their puppies' tails docked, many veterinary surgeons will now refuse to carry out the operation on ethical grounds. This can make life extremely difficult for those JR breeders wishing to continue this practice, and is the cause for much concern among many working dog societies, who argue that working dogs of many types (i.e. not solely terriers) require their tails to be docked to avoid serious injury during the dog's working career.

A rough-coated tan-and-white JR.

In order to lobby for the continuation of legal docking, and to give breeders support and guidance, the Council for Docked Breeds was formed (see appendix).

Some JR breeders are attempting to breed litters with short tails, and it will be interesting to see if this can be achieved consistently and effectively.

Which sex?

Both sexes make good working animals and/or pets, but they also both have their problems, and it is worth considering these before deciding which sex to choose.

Many years ago, when I was considering purchasing my first dog, a good friend and dog trainer gave me sage advice, which I remember to this day. He told me that, while bitches were undoubtedly a nuisance for about four weeks a year, dogs were a nuisance for 52 weeks a year. This is worth considering, and refers to the fact that, when the female comes into season (oestrus) she can be irrational, bad tempered and the proverbial pain (hence the expression used for a cantankerous female human – a bitch). Dogs, however, are always 'in season' and can be troublesome throughout the year.

I have always found bitches to be much more 'biddable' than dogs and, so long as sensible precautions are taken during the bitch's season, no unwanted litters will result.

Some owners prefer to have their JRs – both dogs and bitches – neutered. This, however, obviously limits one's options. Yet again, great thought must be given to this aspect of keeping a JR. Many claim that neutering bitches (spaying) results in a reduced risk of mammary tumours and the prevention of pyometra, while castrated dogs are said by some to be less aggressive and more biddable after their operation. My own experience with such dogs is far too inconclusive to make any such claims.

How to assess the character of your intended purchase

By carefully looking at and examining the parents of your intended puppy, you should gain a great insight into the characters of their offspring. Fierce, aggressive and 'hard' parents will almost certainly produce difficult to handle progeny. A hard JR is not the best of animals to own, and could well result in bad times for all concerned. Even John Russell, who used his dogs for hunting foxes, abhorred hard dogs and refused to keep any such animals. A working dog does not need to be hard, merely hard-working.

When making your choice from a litter, do not choose the ones which rush at you as these animals may turn out to be too aggressive or difficult to handle and control. Neither should you choose the ones which hide in the background or are too frightened to come out of their corner, as fear can also lead to aggression. The best pups will be those who are cautious but inquisitive. Try to tempt these animals to come to you by gently talking to them, perhaps offering small pieces of food or titbits.

We are all rather vain creatures, and appreciate the opportunity to sing our own praises. If you like the JRs that you see, tell the owner. He will undoubtedly be more than pleased at such remarks, often visibly swelling with pride!

Togetherness – JR-style!

The JR is very much a family dog.

Such a compliment is worth more than gold to a true JR person.

When you have chosen your JR, particularly if it is a puppy, take it home and, without overdoing things, make it feel at home. If home is a kennel, make sure that it is properly prepared for your new arrival, and this should include the provision of water and suitable food (always ensure that the breeder has supplied you with details of the pup's diet, because to change it drastically will result in dietary diarrhoea). Remember that your new puppy will have been used to the company and play of siblings and, when he suddenly finds himself without this, he may be rather unsettled. For this reason, it is

The look that captures the hearts of all JR enthusiasts.

advisable to spend time with him before leaving him on his own. This will also set the scene for a healthy rapport in the future.

At what age should your JR be obtained?

Not everyone wants a puppy; for various reasons, some owners will want a dog which has been brought on a little, particularly if that dog is wanted for show or working. There are, of course, both advantages and disadvantages in either course of action, and much thought needs to be given to this aspect of purchasing a JR. Personally, I prefer to take on a puppy at about eight weeks of age, at which stage I feel that I have a better chance of moulding it to my requirements, without inheriting other people's mistakes.

All puppies go through important developmental stages, and you should consider this before making your purchase.

I feel that the best age to buy a puppy is at about eight weeks, because this is the beginning of one of the most crucial stages of the pup's development. Between eight weeks and six months, a young JR will learn about people, animals and its general environment. During this period, they should begin their training (see next chapter). Although they obviously cannot be taught complex tasks at this age, they should still be taught good behaviour (obedience), and this will be the foundation of later training. This is also a period of socialisation, and JRs will benefit greatly from being taken to socialisation classes or 'puppy playgroups' organised by breed clubs, training groups, animal behaviourists and veterinary surgeons. Obviously, your JR should not be taken to any such event until such time as his vaccinations are completed; always check this with your veterinary surgeon, rather than hazarding a guess.

This period of socialisation with his own kind (preferably several different breeds of differing sizes) is extremely important for your JR, if he is not to become fearful of or aggressive towards other dogs. Even if you have several dogs of your own, it is still worthwhile taking your pup to meet other dogs under controlled conditions. Being attacked by an unruly dog in the local park is NOT the way to get your JR to accept other dogs.

Exposure to differing environs, people and occurrences will help you produce a more rounded JR which will face any new situation well, and without embarrassing you or putting people or dogs at risk.

What makes a good JR?

Everyone has their own ideas on this subject, and very few will agree on all aspects. To me, a good JR is one which performs its tasks well – be it a hunter, a pet or a show dog – and is easy to handle, come what may. I do not like hard terriers.

An example of a terrier described as a Jack Russell which may or may not be the reader's ideal.

Some JRs appeal to me because of their looks, i.e. they are aesthetically pleasing *to me*, but remember the old saying 'Beauty is in the eye of the beholder', and different looks appeal to different people. If *you* like the looks of a particular JR, and the way that it behaves – its nature and behaviour – then that will be a good JR for you. If there is one aspect of the JR that you don't like – be it size, colour, or nature – then it is a bad JR *for you*!

Whatever you choose to do when selecting your new JR, always bear in mind the legal phrase *caveat emptor* – buyer beware. Think long and hard before making your decision, and do your homework, tracking down possible suitable JRs from which to make your choice.

Documents

It is always wise to obtain some documentation from the breeder/supplier of a dog. In the case of a pedigree Parson Jack Russell terrier, this should include the relevant Kennel Club registration documents. Sometimes, however, this is not available at the time of purchase, due to delays with the registration process. If this is the case, the vendor must send the documents to the purchaser as soon as they are available.

I always issue a receipt for any puppies or adult dogs which I sell, and always insist on one from those from whom I purchase a dog. To me this is common sense, and a safeguard against the occasional mistake.

I also issue full details of the dog's diet and, if relevant, vaccination and 'Identichipping' certificates are given at the time of purchase.

Identification of JRs

Currently, the Kennel Club does not insist on registered dogs being uniquely identifiable, but I can see the day coming when one or more bodies – including governmental – may well insist on this.

The two main types of permanent identification available to JR owners are tattooing and the implant of a tiny (about the size of a grain of rice) combination of a microchip and an electromagnetic coil, encased in soda lime glass, all of which are totally inert. I favour the Identichip, and all my dogs have one implanted under their skins, in the neck region. This is done via a simple injection which is virtually painless and doesn't result in bleeding of any consequence.

The Identichip responds to a low voltage signal from a special 'reader' and then transmits its unique code, which is displayed by the reader.

Some countries are, at the time of writing, considering the use of DNA profiles (obtained from blood samples) to check against misrepresentation.

Veterinary examination

Today, when JRs can command relatively high prices, it should come as no surprise to learn that many vendors and purchasers insist on their JR being 'vetted' before the purchase can be finalised. This provides a safeguard for all concerned, and should in no way be seen as indicative of mistrust from either party, but rather as a positive move to ensure that all really is as it seems.

As long as one obeys the simple, common sense rules outlined in this chapter, it should not prove difficult to select a good JR, but I am a great believer in going with the heart. If I am faced by a litter in which I have several first-rate candidates from which to choose, I always allow my gut feelings to rule. To date, these feelings have never been disproved.

CHAPTER 3

HOUSING AND TRAINING

Perhaps the first question to ask yourself about your forthcoming new arrival (and, of course, this should be settled *before* the new JR arrives) is where his home is going to be. Many owners are quite happy to allow their canine pets

The eyes have it! A young JR gives its owner a look sure to melt his heart.

the complete run of the human home; others limit the dogs to certain areas, while yet others will not have a dog inside the human home, housing their dog in an outside kennel, run or building. As with everything, the decision is very personal, and each has its good and bad points.

The human home

Allowing one's dog to share the family home is probably the easiest and most popular choice for JRs, especially where only one or two terriers are kept. Even so, it is still worthwhile giving the new puppy a place of its own, where it can retire when it needs to get away from the family, and where it will feel safe. This place should also be one that is safe and out of the way of the human members of the household.

Many JR owners allow their dog to have free run of the whole house, and give the JR a bed to which he can go whenever he or the family wishes. This bed is placed in one of the downstairs rooms, usually the kitchen. This has much to commend it, as most kitchens give easy access to the garden, where your dog will be able to answer nature's calls. Kitchens also, on the whole, have floor coverings which allow for easy cleaning, unlike the other rooms in the home whose floors are invariably covered with carpet.

In your dog's 'bedroom' you should place his bed and bedding, along with a bowl of water. It may also be wise to make this place the one where he eats, and where children are forbidden to go, therefore ensuring that no one will come to harm by interfering with your dog's eating habits. This is particularly important with very young children, since they are more likely to try to torment your dog with his food. If this happens, there can be no point in criticising your dog for reacting to such stimuli, and that reaction may well result in physical harm to the child concerned.

Kennels

Those of us who keep our dogs for working, and so expect a little more than the average obedience, tend to keep the dogs in outside buildings or kennels. To me, this is the best way to keep working dogs, as they are physically separated from the human family and the distractions that they would bring to the dogs.

Kennelling a dog also helps to reduce the inevitable dirt, mud and water associated with JRs and so keeps the peace among members of the human family.

An outside kennel should be such that the dog(s) inside will be comfortable whatever the elements may throw at them. It must be insulated against high and low temperatures, completely water and wind proof, and also durable enough to stand up to the rigours of housing such energetic beasties as JRs. It must also afford the inmates some degree of privacy, and allow them to exhibit much of their natural behavioural repertoire.

The positioning of the kennel is the first potential problem that needs to be tackled. It should be such that it receives some sunshine, without getting the full heat of the midday sun, which will very quickly turn the kennel into an oven, with possibly disastrous consequences. The prevailing winds must not be able to blow directly into the structure, although it is essential that the building has adequate ventilation. A trellis, covered with a non-poisonous creeping plant, will make an attractive and efficient wind break and sun shield, and will be appreciated by the family and neighbours. It must be designed and built with ongoing cleaning and maintenance in mind, but within budget, and it must be large enough for the JRs and for the human cleaner.

If you intend using the kennel for a brood bitch, this should also be borne in mind at the planning stage.

My own kennels are built into large wooden sheds, with outside runs extending out of the sides of the building and into the adjacent field. The

Waste produced by dogs kept in kennels must be disposed of properly. Here, the kennel owner is burning the waste material; in some areas, such fires are not acceptable.

building itself is fifteen metres long, and eight metres wide, and is divided into three kennels, each housing one or more dogs; each of these kennels measures approximately four metres square. A large work area is at the door end of the building, and this consists of a sink, with adequate drainage and hot water via an electric water heater, and various cupboards and such like for storage of feed dishes, leads, collars and other equipment. Brooms, shovels, detergents, buckets and scrubbing brushes are also stored in the building, and a large power hose is available to be fixed to one of two water taps along the walkway, which extends down one side of the building.

The whole building is equipped with fluorescent lighting, which can be operated in zones, while every kennel also has its own fluorescent light as well as a bulkhead light which can be used for lighting a specific kennel while not disturbing dogs in adjacent kennels. This latter light is extremely useful during whelping or when attending to a sick or injured dog.

Inside each kennel is a bed, approximately one metre square, and raised approximately thirty centimetres off the concrete floor. Above this bed is an infra-red heat lamp which can be lowered or raised, and is operated from outside of the kennel.

The roof of the building is under-drawn, and insulated with loft insulation. Ventilation is provided by louvred vents around the walls of the building, any or all of which can be closed off to prevent draughts caused by prevailing winds. Down each side of the building, but not at the end facing the prevailing winds, are windows, glazed with 'unbreakable' polypropylene material, any or all of which may be opened to allow for more ventilation, should the need arise.

The runs from each kennel are as wide as the kennel, and approximately four metres long. They have a concrete base, and the sides are formed from galvanised weld mesh. This weld mesh also extends over the top of the runs and, at the end adjoining the building, the runs have a roof of corrugated clear polypropylene, measuring about one and a half metres, to give shelter to the dogs in adverse weather conditions.

The flooring in the inside kennel and in the runs, slopes towards the outside of the building, where there is a drain, which carries away rainwater and cleaning water etc. to the main drains for the property. This allows the liberal use of hose pipes to ensure a clean area for the dogs, clear of any disinfectant deposits or faecal remains.

We have made very sure that, even were we to employ a man two metres tall, he would still be able to stand and walk around in the runs. There is little more frustrating than constantly bumping one's head on a low roof.

The weld mesh on the runs is mounted onto galvanised posts which are embedded into the concrete, and the weld mesh is raised off the ground by mounting it above a low (approximately fifty centimetres) wall, made from concrete blocks, which are painted with exterior masonry paint. The concrete floors are sealed, to prevent urine and water from sinking into the porous material, and the inside of the kennels and building are painted in a pastel blue gloss paint.

Thought should be given to the colour of the paint used for the insides of buildings and kennels before the paint is purchased. While many are happy to use just any old paint which happens to be lying around, or going cheap, others apply scientific methods to find the best colours. Psychologists have proved that colours such as white and yellow cause animals (and humans) within those buildings to become easily stressed. Dark, dowdy colours, such as black or brown, cause depression, and the best colours for animals seem to be pastel shades of either blue or green. This psychology has even been put into place in hospitals and police and prison cells.

Cleaning

If you are to successfully keep JRs for a long time, it is important that you instigate a sound cleaning regime, using the correct materials and tools, at the very start of your project. As mentioned earlier, this is far easier to achieve if you plan the design properly, and give great thought to the materials used in the construction of the kennels.

Dogs, by their nature, are extremely clean animals; they spend much time on personal hygiene, and can be very particular where they empty their bladders and bowels. When taken to the garden to relieve themselves, puppies can be taught to use just one area (see under toilet training), and the same methods can be utilised within a kennel.

A good quality disinfectant should be used to help reduce the build up of smells and harmful bacteria, but great care is needed in the choice of disinfectant. Disinfectant agents are classed as either physical or chemical, for example steam can be used to clean cages, and is commonly used in commercial kennels and catteries. Steam is a physical agent, whereas chemical agents are found in the disinfectants which we can buy from many High Street outlets. All disinfectants are potentially dangerous, and yet their labelling would often lead one to believe otherwise! Some are highly toxic to certain species, while all can cause allergic reactions in certain individuals. All disinfectants work better at higher temperatures, and so should be mixed with hot water to form a solution of the correct ratio. NEVER mix two disinfectants together, as the results could be highly dangerous.

The chemicals used in disinfectants are classified into generic groups – alcohols, aldehydes, alkalis, halogens, phenolics and surface-active agents – and common disinfectants draw their constituents from the aldehydes (e.g. formalin), the halogens (e.g. sodium hypochlorite – bleach), and the phenolics (e.g. phenol). In addition, the surface-active agents are sub-divided into two more groups – quaternary ammonium compounds ('quats'), and amphoteric/polymer surface-active agents. The latter group is the one which contains the most recently developed disinfectants, which act as both detergents and disinfectants, making them excellent for both cleaning surfaces and then rendering them 'safe'. I cannot recommend highly enough the use of these preparations in kennels and all areas frequented by your JR

There are two generic types of disinfectant generally available – sodium hypochlorite (bleach) and phenol.

Bleach

This is extremely effective and forms the basis of many cleaners and disinfectants, all of which are cheap, easily available and, providing that common sense precautions are taken, relatively safe and, therefore, useful for cleaning kennels etc. Sodium hypochlorite has a very low residual toxicity and it is used throughout the world for cleaning dairy utensils and milking machines etc. It can, therefore, in addition to being used for cleaning the kennel itself, obviously be used for cleaning the JRs' dishes and drinking bottles, provided that these are well rinsed before use.

It should be noted that all disinfectants are only effective when used on cleaned and rinsed surfaces, as even small amounts of detergent or organic material can inactivate sodium hypochlorite. Solutions of bleach and water, if left standing for any time, will also lose their efficacy, as the bleach oxidises, and much is lost to the atmosphere. Because of this, it is important that all bleach solutions are used immediately they are prepared; if they are left standing, they will be totally ineffective against micro-organisms, and you may as well save your money and simply use a bucket of water.

After using bleaches in kennels and such areas, all surfaces must be rinsed well with clean water, and then allowed to stand empty for about 30 minutes, before returning the JRs to the area.

Phenol

Popularly known as carbolic acid, phenol is a caustic poison which is extremely toxic to living tissue. Modern derivatives (all of which share the same properties as phenol) include xylenol, chloroxyphenol, ortho-phenylphenol and hexachlorophene, and are equally dangerous to living tissue, being absorbed through the skin. An indication of the inherent danger of their use is that many of these substances have been banned from use in all products designed for human babies, and have long been forbidden in catteries. When used in kennels, the inhabitants may well suffer from sore feet, tails and tummies, and even 'burns' to their lips, mouth and tongues.

It is easy to tell if a disinfectant contains phenol, as it will turn white when added to water. I would strongly recommend that no such materials are used when cleaning kennels and other areas frequented by your JR, as the risks are just too great.

In the UK and most other countries, the labels on most disinfectant bottles and containers will list the chemical ingredients. However, in some countries, this is not so, and it is possible to see manufacturers' claims that the substance is 'safe', 'safe in use', or 'safe when used as directed'. I have never seen any label which claims that the disinfectant is safe for use with all animals and, even if this were true, there could still be individual animals which have an allergy to one or more of the chemical ingredients in the product.

Many disinfectants have added 'smell', usually pine or similar; while this may make the liquid more appealing to humans, it will only mask smells. Of course, if the JR's kennel is properly and regularly cleaned, there will be no need for masking! In addition, heat (from heaters or even the sun) may well cause irritant fumes to be drawn from untreated timber into which the disinfectant has soaked.

Whichever disinfectant you use, ensure that you adhere strictly to the manufacturer's recommended dilutions and, if any animal shows signs of an allergic reaction – change the disinfectant immediately.

Cleaning utensils

Obviously, in order to carry out the day-to-day cleaning of the kennel – essential to avoid health problems – certain items of equipment are needed. These need not be elaborate, and most homes will already have most items 'in stock'. However, it is advisable to have a totally separate set of cleaning utensils, which are to be used exclusively for the kennels and runs used by your JR. In larger kennels, and even where only two or three JRs are kept, it is highly recommended that a separate set is used for each kennel, in order to reduce the risks of cross-infection, and that interchange of utensils does not occur. General items that you will require are listed below:

Hard bristled, long handled broom
Hard bristled hand brush
Dust pan/shovel
Scraper (for cleaning solid waste trodden into floor etc; a paint scraper is
    ideal)
Buckets (stainless steel are best, although plastic will suffice)
High power hose pipe (or, even better, a pressure washer – see below)
Scrubbing brushes (deck scrubbing brushes, with long handles, are ideal for
    kennels)

Pressure washers are designed to operate at either high or low pressures, using hot or cold water, or steam, and most can be fitted with a device to spray a mixture of water and cleaner or disinfectant. They are ideal for cleaning kennels – roof, walls and floors.

Try to establish a routine, which will help you, and also ensure that the JRs have well cleaned kennels, thus helping them lead longer and healthier – and dare I say happier – lives. To reduce the risk of smells, keep two buckets by the door of the cage, one containing a mild solution of surface action cleaner, and the other fresh water; both buckets will require cleaning out and replenishing every few days. As the dirty feeding bowls are removed from the kennels, I wash and rinse them in the buckets, before replacing them in their storage cupboards.

Just waiting to be slipped – a JR eagerly awaits an afternoon's work.

Flies are always a nuisance in warm weather, and they are best tackled by keeping a strict cleaning regime, regularly clearing all soiled areas. In addition, suspending fly papers around the outside of the kennel will help reduce the problem. Even where flies are a great nuisance, one should *never* use insecticidal sprays in or around an occupied kennel.

Food and water dishes

Water is essential for all animals, and you should always make sure that your JR can get to a constant supply of clean, fresh drinking water. Dishes can easily be tipped up – even quite heavy ones – and the water may soon become fouled and undrinkable, even if the dish is emptied, cleaned and replenished daily.

Some JRs seem to enjoy hurling their dishes around the kennel, spilling the contents in so doing. To get around this problem, we use drinking nipples which we first saw in a pig unit on a local farm. The nipples are connected to a watering system which is fed, via hidden piping, from a cistern to each kennel. This ensures that water is always available, and is clean and of drinking quality.

All bowls used should be cleaned after each use, using a top quality disinfectant/detergent, and then stored safely until next needed. We only use stainless steel bowls. Our dogs will chew plastic bowls, given half a chance, and ceramic or pot bowls have too much potential to be broken. Always err on the side of safety, even if this involves a bit more expense. We are great believers in buying the best we can, in the knowledge that, over time, this will actually save us money.

Heaters

Any heaters used anywhere that a JR can get to must be made safe. I would advise that, in a kennel, all heaters are raised off the ground, with all wires concealed behind walls, or else protected from inquisitive teeth by the use of metal or similar piping. As mentioned earlier, we use overhead, infra-red bulbs, and these are fitted with large reflectors. The height of the bulbs can easily be adjusted, and they are fitted with a dimmer switch, which allows us to have them on a low heat setting.

Waste disposal

It can come as no surprise to readers that some members of the public simply do not like dogs. These people will use any excuse to attack dog-owners, and their stepping into a pile of dog faeces will simply give them ammunition. It is incumbent on us all to ensure that we clean up after our dogs. I am always amazed and saddened by the number of dog owners who just couldn't care less, and leave their dogs' mess where it is. Not only is this the case for the pet owner, but also for many professionals.

Throughout the year, I give demonstrations and displays with various animals – ferrets, dogs, hawks etc. – and often find myself on the same programme as some dog display – gundogs, racing terriers, agility etc. While many of these demonstrators make a big thing of *saying* that we must all be responsible pet owners, many of them do not practise what they preach. This is made all too clear for me when, in the middle of my display, I quite literally put my foot in it! If these people are not willing to clean up after their dogs when they are in the public eye, I very much doubt that they will clean up at other times.

It is simplicity itself to 'scoop the poop'; all that is needed is a plastic bag or two, a little thought, and a little effort. Once you have returned to base with your JR and put him safely away, dispose of the poop by dropping it in the dustbin. Where larger numbers of JRs are kept, and also where a considerable amount of waste is produced, other methods of disposing safely of the material must be found.

A large 'incinerator' is often the best and most economic method, providing

How not to dispose of waste material. Piles of rubbish such as this are a health risk, and will positively encourage rats and other vermin.

that thought is given to the smoke produced by such a device. Ensure that this smoke will not adversely affect neighbours before lighting the fire.

Noise

While JRs' barks and yaps may well help dissuade burglars and other nefarious visitors, the noise can also upset neighbours. Yet it would be insane to think that there was any way of stopping the noise; we need to minimise its effect.

A high fence or hedge, between the kennels and the neighbours' gardens will work as a kind of baffle, and will have a significant effect on the amount of noise pollution allowed to escape to upset people. Hedges can always look pretty, especially if several different hedging bushes are used, while fences can be planted with climbers and other such plants to give a very pleasing effect. None of this, however, should be seen as an excuse for not trying to prevent your JRs barking endlessly throughout the day and night.

Training your JR

Barbara Woodhouse is famous for stating that 'there is no such thing as a bad dog, merely bad owners of dogs', and I heartily concur with that sentiment. Personally, the things I hate most in life are bad drivers, badly behaved children, and badly behaved dogs. In the last two, the fault does not lie entirely with the child or the dog, but with the 'trainers', i.e. the child's parents and the dog's owners. Unfortunately, I also believe that 90% of humans will never make good dog trainers.

This should not, however be taken as an excuse for anyone having a badly behaved dog. If you realise that you can't train the animal correctly on your own – seek help.

DIY versus classes

With some people, it is relatively straightforward to buy a book or video on a subject, and then simply get on with it. I know of many people who proudly boast that they are entirely self-taught. But this brings back to me an old saying passed on to me by a professor of zoology – 'the person who is self-taught has had a fool for a teacher'. Far better, to my mind, to have at least a few lessons with a professional dog trainer. That way, you will be shown the correct methods to use, while also being put right when you make a mistake. After all, a good trainer trains both the dog *and* its owner. Unless this is done, no matter how well-trained the dog, a bad trainer/owner will inevitably ruin all of the good work put into it.

Once you have had your lessons, it is easy to neglect the on-going training and development of the dog. When people visit me and ask if I have any 'fully trained' dogs for sale, I try to explain to them that no dog is ever 'fully trained', requiring on-going attention and practice to keep the dog working well. One of the best ways to ensure that you do keep up this work is to join a training class.

Experienced handlers have many 'tricks of the trade' to ensure that their charge shows his or her best to the judge.

Types of classes

There are many types of class, and you should spend time looking at each one on offer before finally committing to any one of them. Some classes are run by clubs, and insist on everyone being a full member before they can take part. Some classes are intended only for one specific breed, or one discipline, such as agility or ring work. Obviously, then, you need to have a good idea of what *you* want out of the class before enrolling.

A good place to start your enquiries is your breed club or your local veterinary surgery; most vets are only too pleased to have cards and posters on display in their waiting room. Take a pen and paper along with you and note down the ones which appear interesting to you. Once you have made this short-list, speak to the head nurse, and see if she knows of any, and can give you more details.

Next, prepare a list of questions to which you will need answers, in order to help you make your final decision. They should include the following:

> What types/breeds of dog are catered for?
> What is actually taught at the classes?
> What qualifications do the instructors hold?
> Are they suitable for beginners?
> What time and day of the week are they held?
> Do you need to join a club to attend the classes?
> How much will the classes cost?
> Can you attend one and see if you like it, without having to commit to long-term participation?

Once you have spoken to all of the class organisers on your list, make a pot of coffee and sit down to think things through. Discuss your thoughts with your partner or a friend, and then make a preference list. This list should be headed by the class which you believe is the best for you, and then the other suitable classes listed in order of preference. Once you have made your mind up, ring and make arrangements to attend the class.

The class

When making arrangements to attend the class, ask what equipment you should take with you. Some classes insist on everyone using, for instance, a specific kind of training collar; some insist on your taking edible treats for your dog. Don't forget your poop scoop!

Give yourself plenty of time to get to the class, so that you aren't all hot and bothered at the beginning of the class; this will not be conducive to a good class.

Enjoyment

Dog training should be fun for everyone involved, including the dogs, and joining a good class will enable you to make the most of having your pet. It will also help you to get your dog socialised, an important part of its development. Without socialisation, your dog will never be happy in the company of other dogs, and may even attack them. Even older dogs can be helped in this respect with the proper training and environment, both of which will be available at a good class run by competent instructors.

Even though it may seem hard work at first, and even if, after a few sessions, you feel that neither you nor your dog is making progress, stick with it. Everything takes time. Think how proud you will feel walking through the park with a perfectly behaved dog, and knowing that you have enjoyed yourself and made friends while achieving this. It will all be worthwhile and both you and your dog – not to mention other members of the family, friends, neighbours and even the general public – will have better lives for it.

Equipment

There is an old saying – 'You cannot teach an old dog new tricks'. This is not true, you can, providing that you are extremely patient and, of course, it will take more time. You will also need knowledge, skill and equipment. The minimum equipment that you will require to train your JR is a lead and a collar.

There are many different types of lead, and the choice is a personal one. Some trainers prefer nylon, some rope, and others leather. The length and thickness are also important; I prefer a nylon lead, about two metres long and 20 mm thick. Because I am prone to putting them down in 'safe' places or even dropping them, I always choose brightly coloured leads – red for preference.

When it comes to collars, there are many schools of thought. A modern one is that you should always 'be kind', and use a collar which cannot hurt your dog, such as a normal leather collar. Another school states quite simply that no-one can ever train a JR! While, to a degree, I can empathise with the last statement, I feel that we should all try to train our dogs in basic obedience at the very least.

Consequently, I favour a check chain, of about 15 mm thickness, although on some of my dogs, I use rope checks. When fitted and used properly, this is very effective and will not harm the dog on which it is fitted. Unfortunately, many dog owners cannot do this, and so, as stated earlier, I would suggest that expert help and guidance is sought. The photograph on page 66 shows the correct way to fit a check chain.

A good example of a black-and-white JR.

All dog training is about association of ideas, and all training sessions should be short but often. Never risk boring your dog, or you will become frustrated by his apparent inability to carry out 'simple' tasks. Be consistent in your actions and commands, and make the exercises fun for both of you. Get your instructions and guidance before bad habits develop, as training should be about establishing acceptable behaviour and not simply for breaking bad habits. At all times, *you* must be the boss, the alpha male, or very soon, anarchy – or worse – will occur.

Training the puppy to come to you on command

All animal training is linked to association of ideas, or conditioned reflexes; the reaction that the animal is conditioned to exhibit when it receives a certain stimulus. The great Russian physiologist, Ivan Pavlov, investigated conditioned reflexes in his famous experiments of the late 19th and early 20th centuries. He noticed that he could induce the production of saliva in dogs by the sight, smell and taste of food; he then linked the appearance of food with an external stimulus – a bell ringing. After a while, he found that saliva production could be induced simply by ringing the bell.

One of the first things that the puppy must be taught is his own name. This should never be used to call the dog to you, merely as a way of getting his attention, in the same way that a school teacher will call out the name of the pupil to get their attention before they are given a task. The way I do this is through a treat.

I get a piece of wholemeal bread, about 25 mm square and, as the puppy is playing, I wait for him to turn away from me, at which point I call his name. As soon as he turns towards me, I say 'nicely', and proffer the bread towards him. After a few sessions like this, some of which do not utilise a treat but a cuddle instead, the puppy will react to his name. This needs to be incorporated into all further training sessions, and the puppy's name should prefix all of the commands in the following exercises. The importance of this will only really become apparent where the household has several dogs, and the trainer wishes only one of them to carry out a specific command.

Walking on a lead

Have you ever marvelled at how many people are prepared to allow their dogs to take them for a drag? I would find such an experience anything but relaxing, and would never consider having any dogs which I could not take out on a lead without having my arm wrenched from its socket. A little time and effort, early on in the JR's life, will soon have the little chap walking nicely at heel. Every dog should be trained to walk nicely on a lead, and a lead should always

An elderly JR who still manages to put in a full day's work.

be used whenever the dog is being walked near a public road, for obvious safety reasons.

Obviously, the dog will not take to the lead instantly, and so the training should start slowly, and as soon as possible.

Use a collar that is soft but strong (never a check chain at this stage), made from either leather or nylon. Every collar I have bought has required new holes for secure fastening, and I find a special leather hole punch to be an indispensable aid for this operation. Place the collar around your JR's neck, and mark the place where the hole needs to be. Once you have punched the hole, you can try the collar on the JR to ensure that you have it right. There should be room for two fingers to fit fairly snugly under the collar, without choking the dog. Once fitted, place the JR on the floor; he will immediately try his hardest to get the collar off, and so he should be distracted for 5–10 minutes, by which time he will have forgotten the collar, and will thus accept it.

When this has happened – and not before – it is time to attach the lead to the collar. Again, the JR will react to the new encumbrance, and so requires distraction until such time as it is accepted. Once this is achieved, you are ready to embark on your first walk together. Don't be too ambitious; a 30-mile route march will not be a happy occasion for the JR or yourself. The first few walks should be taken at a very leisurely pace, and not cover more than a few hundred metres. Your puppy will no doubt dig his heels in, and, even when walking, will keep stopping at every new smell and sight. Try to make the whole experience of the walk a pleasurable one, for both of you. Be patient and remember that the things which you take for granted, and to which you react in a blasé manner, will be entirely new and mysterious – maybe even frightening – to your puppy.

Once your puppy will walk in this manner without pulling too much (if he does pull, give a short, sharp yank which should be directed straight down his back, along the direction of his spine to his tail), saying 'NO!' at the same time. He will soon get the idea.

Do not take the puppy onto public areas, paths or roads until all of his vaccinations are completed, and he has been given the all-clear by the vet.

Once your puppy will walk reasonably well on a lead without constantly digging in his heels and having to be dragged, it is time to move to the check collar. I know of many owners of JRs who use chain checks, and also some who use rope checks; both will work if fitted and used correctly by the handler.

I insist on all my dogs walking on my left-hand side (probably because of all the gundogs I train), and I would recommend this to every trainer. The dog needs to have consistency, otherwise he may well keep crossing from side to side and, inevitably, end up by tripping you on the lead.

Fit the collar and lead as normal, and then walk the puppy along. After

20–30 metres, say 'SIT', and immediately stop. Take up the slack in the lead (which should at all other times be slack), and ensure that the puppy stops alongside you. He must learn that when you stop, he stops, and that when you say 'Sit', he stops. This is arguably the most important lesson that your puppy must learn, since a timely 'SIT!' will get him and you out of serious trouble.

Make him stop for a few seconds, and then walk on, giving him the command 'HEEL', in a nice, friendly voice. After a few more metres, give the 'SIT' command again, and repeat the whole exercise. After two of these 'stop and go' sessions, I always give the pup a bit of free exercise, as indeed I do before the start of every training period.

The exercise can be reinforced at feeding time. Put your puppy on his check and lead, and walk him away from his feeding area. While you are doing this, get a friend to place the puppy's meal in its usual place (which will be behind you and the puppy at the time). Once this is done, stop the pup, turn him, and walk him at heel towards the meal. When he sees or smells the food, he will become excited and start to pull. Do not let him! Keep him at heel, and stop him about one metre away from the food dish. Make him sit and wait for a few seconds, and then, while still on the lead tell him 'NICELY', and allow him to move forward and eat his meal. Repeat this at each meal time, and soon the puppy will automatically sit when his food dish appears.

A young undocked JR.

Toilet training

Arguably one of – if not *the*– first bits of training for any puppy, particularly if he is to share the human home, toilet or house training can be extremely stressful for all concerned, although it need not be.

The first thing to do is to decide where you will want your new puppy to 'do his business'. If it is in the human home, you may wish him to use a litter tray, or a specific corner of the room, into which you have placed copious amounts of old newspapers. On the other hand, it would seem more satisfactory, particularly in the long term, if your puppy was taught, from day one, to use an outside latrine. This will probably be in the garden, and so it is best if the puppy is taught only to use a single place in the garden.

This is best achieved by selecting an appropriate place, and then, using weld mesh or chicken mesh, fence off a small area. Every time you take your puppy out to relieve himself, you should carry him to this spot, place him inside the wired area, and then stay with him until such time as he has performed his duties. If this routine is adhered to every time, then in later life, your JR will only use the one area for his toilet.

It is possible to refine this state of affairs even more. As your puppy is relieving himself, say a word which you have chosen for him to associate with this action, for example 'squirt'. When your puppy has finished, praise him in a happy voice. Very soon he will realise what is expected of him when the word is said, and will, if he needs to, relieve himself on command. Conversely, if you should catch your puppy relieving himself in the wrong place, say a stern 'NO!', pick him up immediately, and carry him to his allocated toilet area, where you should use your word of command to encourage him to finish his toilet there. Do not move him out of this area until such time as he has performed.

It is important that you only admonish your puppy at the actual time at which he is doing wrong; dogs cannot associate current actions with things that happened even a few seconds ago. For this reason, you should never admonish or punish the dog as he comes towards you, even if it is immediately after he has committed a crime. To do so will mean that the puppy will associate this punishment with his last action, i.e. coming to you. If your puppy runs away from you, and will not come back to the recall command, shout his name to get his attention and, immediately he looks at you, run off in the opposite direction, giving the recall as you go. Dogs will always follow the alpha male (pack leader) and, provided you have established yourself as such, he will follow you. Even though you may be extremely angry with your puppy, do not speak harshly to him, or punish him in any way whatsoever, for the reason previously discussed. Instead, praise him for coming to you. Often, in order to vent my frustration and anger, I use harsh words to my dog, but in a very friendly and happy way: therefore, as no dog can understand every word that humans use, rather being influenced by manner, tone and intonation, he will feel very happy at what he believes are his pleasing actions towards the boss.

There are many other training tasks that one will need to undertake during the dog's career, but at this stage, you should be establishing the foundations for all later training, and it is vital that these foundations are rock solid. Any corners cut at this stage, or lessons not properly taught by yourself and learned by your puppy, will rebound on you later, causing great consternation, worry and heartache.

CHAPTER 4

FEEDING

To many people, the feeding of their pets is a matter that is given very little thought; as long as 'food' can be obtained at the right price, the matter is rarely – if ever – discussed. However, the correct diet – balanced to give the right amounts of the relevant constituents – is essential for the long and healthy life of every animal. As our JRs are extremely important to us, so should their diet be. Before discussing what we should feed our dogs on, it is worthwhile looking at just what makes a 'balanced diet'. Once this is understood, and the importance of and reason for each constituent in that diet, we will be better placed to ensure that, whatever life style, life stage, fitness or illness our JR may be enduring at any time, we can supply a diet that will help the animal.

A balanced diet

All animals require certain items in their diet, with quite large differences between species. All animals require water, fat/carbohydrate, protein, fibre, some minerals and some vitamins. A JR fed on a truly balanced diet should lead a long, active and healthy life, be able to play and run and, if relevant, work and, therefore, more than repay you for the cost of its diet. The main components of any diet are proteins, vitamins, minerals, carbohydrates, fats and fibre.

Proteins
Proteins, made from amino acids, are essential for growth and tissue building and repair. They are present in meats, eggs and milk. There are many different proteins, all consisting of different arrangements of about 20 amino acids, but it is not necessary to differentiate between them here.

It should be obvious that, while JRs require a high protein diet, this is even more important when considering nursing mothers, their pups and young JRs in general. Likewise, males used for stud also require a higher protein content in their diet.

Carbohydrates

Carbohydrates provide the body with energy, from which it can produce heat and material for growth. Carbohydrates are made up of carbon, hydrogen and oxygen (which combine to form cellulose, starch and sugar), and excess amounts are stored as fat in the body, often leading to obesity. As everyone knows, this can cause medical problems and difficulties in the JR's breeding, whether it be a male or female. Also, an overweight dog will not be as active, nor as agile as he should be, and so will not be as happy.

Vitamins

Vitamins are chemical compounds, essential for growth, health, normal metabolism, and general physical well-being. Many vitamins play an important part in completing essential chemical reactions in the body, forming parts of enzymes, which act as chemical catalysts. Some vitamins form parts of hormones, which are the chemical substances that regulate specific functions in the body, including reproduction. There are two main types of vitamin – water-soluble and fat-soluble.

Water-soluble vitamins cannot be stored in the body, and so the day's food must contain the day's requirements of these vitamins. Fat-soluble vitamins can be stored in the body and, if too many are taken in at one time, they can be stored for use when the body needs them. However, an excess of such vitamins may cause toxic levels to accumulate in storage areas such as the liver. It is important to remember that an excess of any fat-soluble vitamin can lead to long-term physical problems. You should also remember that a lack of essential vitamins can be detrimental to the dog's health.

In summary, the 'average' JR requires a diet comprising:

Protein (25%) – for tissue and muscle growth and repair
Fat (20%) – for heating the body, and providing energy
Calcium (10%) – for teeth and bones
Phosphorous (1%) – for teeth and bones
Salt (1%) – a vital mineral which acts as an electrolyte regulating the balance of water inside and outside cells
Fibre (5%) – as an aid to digestion
Daily vitamin requirements (based on dog's weight in kilograms):
Vitamin A (240 IU/kg) – for vision, general growth and healthy skin
Vitamin B1 (15 mg/kg) – aids the nervous system, and aids carbohydrate metabolism
Vitamin B2 (25 mg/kg) – for cell growth
Vitamin B3 (30 mg/kg) – for cell growth and development
Vitamin B5 (50 mg/kg) – aids the nervous system, and aids carbohydrate metabolism

Vitamin B6 (10 mg/kg) – aids general metabolism
Vitamin B12 (0.5 mg/kg) – aids the development of the red blood cells
Vitamin C (50 mg/kg) – for healthy skin and aids wound healing and tissue repair
Vitamin D3 (26.4 IU/kg) – aids calcium and phosphorous metabolism, essential for good bones and teeth; also aids general growth
Vitamin E (about 70 mg/kg) – promotes normal growth and development, acts as an anti-blood clotting agent, and promotes normal red blood cell production.

Vitamin E is found in the yolk of eggs, and in certain vegetable oils. A lack of this vitamin can cause infertility, heart and circulation problems and skin complaints.

Fats and carbohydrates provide the dog's body with energy but, if overfed, the body will store excess in the tissue. This can lead to many problems, including mating difficulties, heart problems and the re-absorption of foetuses. Fats are approximately 2½ times higher in calories, gram for gram, than carbohydrates.

Fibre (or roughage, as it used to be called) is essential for the well-being of the dog's digestive system. Fibre will keep the dog 'regular' and this will help prevent many of the diseases – including cancer of the bowel – with which some dogs may become afflicted.

The mineral calcium is found in liver, milk and milk products, eggshells, fish, and snails. It is also to be found in the bones and teeth of all animals. Phosphorous is found in liver, milk and milk products, and fish. Dogs require a calcium to phosphorous ratio of about 1.3 to 1.

Water

Without sufficient quantities of good, clean drinking water, animal life is impossible, and a shortage of water will kill an animal far more quickly than a shortage of any other constituent of the animal's diet. Water is essential for many functions of the body. It is used as a transport medium (blood); for heat loss (evaporation), elimination of waste products (urine), chemical reactions within the body (digestion and within the blood cells) and many other essential functions. Water is lost as a result of everyday life, and this must obviously be replaced; it is therefore, essential that your JR has constant access to an adequate supply of good, clean drinking water.

The dog's requirement for water, and other nutrients, will be dependent on several factors, including ambient temperatures, life style, age and, in the case of water, diet. Regular checks must be made on all water, especially in extremes of weather. During periods of very low temperatures, the water

Owners line up their dogs prior to a terrier race at a British country fair.

in bowls or pipes may well freeze, and thus the water is unavailable to the JR. In hot weather, the dog will obviously drink far more than normal, and may well empty his dish unless it is kept topped up by you.

Diets

Dogs are carnivores, a word derived from the Latin *carnis*, meaning flesh, and *vorare*, to devour. As such, their natural diet is one of flesh, i.e. whole carcasses of mammals and birds etc. Until twenty or so years ago, most dogs were fed on table scraps, i.e. food left over from human meals. Today, the dog owner has a plethora of feeds from which to choose a suitable one, i.e. one which suits the dog and his owner's pocket. To help the reader make the correct choice, I will explain some of the terms used by dog feed manufacturers in the UK.

A 'complete feed' is defined by AAFCO (the Association of American Feed Control Officials), as 'a nutritionally adequate feed for animals other than man; by specific formula (is) compounded to be fed as the sole ration and (is) capable of maintaining life and/or for promoting production without any additional substance being consumed except water'. This type of food, therefore, can be fed as the dog's staple diet and, apart from giving the dog water, no other nutrient or food need be given. Some foods, however, are not designed to be the staple, but need other items added to them if they are to provide a balanced diet for the dog; these are known as complementary feeds. The United Kingdom Feedingstuffs Regulations (1979), define a 'complementary feedingstuff' as 'a compound feedingstuff which, by reason of its composition, is not sufficient to ensure a daily ration unless it is used in combination with other feedingstuffs'.

In addition, there are different types of both complementary and complete foods. A 'dry' food must contain no more than 12% of water, and is preserved by drying the feed. 'Semi-moist' feeds can contain between 15 and 50% water, and are preserved by the use of humectants, mould inhibitors, and ensuring a low pH (acidity). Canned foods can contain as much as 85% water, and are preserved by heat sterilisation. Frozen foods, obviously preserved by freezing, contain between 60 and 80% water. 'Chub', where the food is preserved by either heat treatment, preservatives or both, contains between 70 and 85% water, and 'plastic pot food', which is preserved by heat sterilisation, contains between 75 and 85% water.

In addition, it is still possible to buy fresh meat, often minced, from pet stores, supermarkets, local butchers and other such outlets. In the UK, it is common to see such meats labelled 'For Animal Feed Only. Not For Human Consumption'.

Each of these food types has its advantages and disadvantages, and each has its adherents. I feed my dogs on a top quality complete dry feed, although I usually start puppies off on tinned dog food, then mix it with soaked complete dry feed, then soaked complete dry feed only. I never feed dry feed dry; I always mix in water, and then leave it to stand for 10–15 minutes. In cold weather, I use hot water which will obviously need to cool enough before being offered to the dogs. Feeding dry feed dry will cause the dog to gorge itself on water, and this will lead to a swollen and very uncomfortable stomach for the dog.

When a dog is ill, or recuperating, he will require a light diet. This should consist of cooked chicken, fish and rice, and plenty of water. When a dog is ill, little and often should be the rule for feeding.

Other foods

Raw green tripe, the unprocessed stomachs of cows, is an excellent food for dogs. In some countries, it is easily obtainable, with some pet shops selling it in 'tubes', minced, frozen and even in tins. However, since the BSE ('mad cow disease') outbreaks in the UK, it has become very difficult to obtain large quantities of green tripe directly from abattoirs, although the situation does seem to be getting easier at the time of writing this book.

Green tripe has a very strong and disagreeable smell; many people will not feed it, solely for this reason. Dogs, however, are not deterred by the smell, and will eat it with gusto. As with all meats, always ensure the tripe is fresh and, if frozen, defrost thoroughly, feeding it as soon afterwards as possible.

Heart, lights (lungs), cheek and udder can be bought reasonably cheaply, and make good dog food, but again its availability is being limited by the BSE scares. Liver is enjoyed by all dogs, and has much nutritional value; however, it should not be fed in excess and NEVER form a staple. Avoid liver, often sold as 'pet food', which has been branded as 'unfit for human consumption', for whatever reason. My personal maxim is that, if liver is not fit for me to eat, it is not fit for my animals either.

Many butchers, supermarkets, pet stores, and other retailers sell 'minced pet food'. This usually consists of many different sorts of meat minced up together and frozen, and will often include offal, fat and waste. It is an open invitation for harmful bacteria; therefore it must be fed immediately after it has been properly defrosted. If you are in any doubt as to its suitability, boil it for at least fifteen minutes before feeding it. These meats also tend to be high in fats, and should not be fed as a staple, although the high fat content will be useful in cold weather, or when the JRs are working hard, as their calorific needs will be much higher than normal.

Fish is relished by many dogs but should only be fed in limited quantities; avoid smoked, salty or fatty fish. All fish must be well filleted, as fish bones can easily become lodged in a dog's wind pipe, often with fatal results.

Eggs

Eggs, in moderation, are good for dogs, giving a nice sheen to the coat, and containing many nutrients. However, too many raw eggs (i.e. more than two or three each week) may have a bad effect on your JR. Feeding too many raw eggs can cause diarrhoea and even hair loss. Try feeding hard boiled or even scrambled eggs. Your dogs will love them, and in this form, they will have no detrimental effect on your JR.

Adjusting the diet

Don't forget that the animal's diet will have to be adjusted to compensate for its lifestyle; a JR kept indoors and not given much exercise will need far less energy food (i.e. fat) than an animal kept outside and worked regularly. All animals will need more fat in colder weather. The mammalian body, through a process known as homeostasis, requires energy (obtained from its food) to maintain its body temperature, and keep all of its organs functioning correctly.

Pregnant and nursing bitches and puppies and young dogs will require higher amounts of protein and calcium. The protein is for body building and general growth, while the calcium is essential for good, strong teeth and bones.

All dogs should be fed daily, and fasted on one day each week; with my own dogs, this is usually on Sundays. A fasting day is good for the health of all animals – including human beings – as it gives the body a rest and a chance to recuperate from any excesses. Obviously, where the dog is working hard on a daily basis, or in the case of pregnant, or nursing bitches or puppies and very young dogs, no fasting should take place.

How much food should a JR be given each day? This is a very difficult question to answer, as it will vary from season to season, and from day to day, depending on ambient temperatures, energy expended by the dog, and many other factors. A general rule of thumb is to feed the dog with an amount which you think is correct, and then check on the food about a half an hour later. If all of the food has been eaten, feed a little extra next time. Ideally, there should still be a small amount of food left about thirty minutes after putting the food down, although where several dogs or puppies are feeding in the same kennel, or even from the same dish, this competitiveness may cause the animals to eat more than they actually need or, indeed, really want.

Check the condition of the dog regularly, by running a finger down the spine. If you can't feel the individual vertebrae easily, this is due to subcutaneous fat, and the animal is therefore overweight, having been fed too much. If, on the other hand, the vertebrae feel extremely sharp, the animal is not being fed enough, and is underweight. In all cases where a JR is eating good quantities of good quality feed, but is still underweight, veterinary advice must be sought. While it is possible that this is due to an infestation of worms (see chapter 8), it may possibly be something more serious. It is always best to err on the side of caution.

As the dog's digestive system, like that of all carnivores, is quite short, too large a quantity of food will result in much of it passing undigested through the dog. Too much food can also cause dietary diarrhoea.

Always remember that variety is the spice of life; whatever diet you decide to feed your JRs, vary it from time to time. This will keep the dogs happy and healthy, and they will return the favour by working and playing even harder! A well-thought out, properly balanced diet will help keep your dogs free from illness and disease. While this is obviously good for JRs, it is also good for you, as it will mean less trouble and fewer vets' bills.

CHAPTER 5

BREEDING

Why breed?

Before embarking on any project, it is always wise to ask yourself why you are doing it, and what you wish to achieve from that project. Where the breeding of animals is concerned, even more thought must be given, as any actions in such a project will involve the lives of animals. Also, if the project is successful, the number of animals will increase, often drastically.

Therefore, the breeding of your Jack Russells is obviously a project which requires long and careful consideration, and must always be carried out for a valid reason. For most of us, that valid reason is the continuing quest for our elusive goal – the 'perfect' JR. As to what actually constitutes such an animal, that depends on what you wish to use the JR for. If you are showing your terrier, you will want to produce a line of JRs which perfectly match the show standards for the organisation under which you will be showing. If you are working your JR, you will no doubt have your own ideas about what will and will not be acceptable to you. However, I am of the opinion that, at least where Jack Russells are concerned, it is possible to have a good-looking terrier that can also carry out a full day in the job for which it was intended. This to me is the main tenet to which all JR breeders must adhere.

Some people are opposed to the breeding of animals because, so they say, money is the prime motive behind such an exercise. As readers will know, this is simply not the case; we wish to improve the breed and produce more top class Jack Russells.

Do you really want to breed from your JR?

Among the questions you should ask yourself at this stage are:

1. Do you have the space for a bitch and her litter of puppies (which may be with you for six months or more)?

It's hard work educating the public. A JR on the Parson Jack Russell Club stand at the 'Discover Dogs' area of Cruft's.

2. Do you have the time to devote to the bitch during and after the birth, and then the puppies, which will need much socialising, cleaning up after, feeding and other often onerous chores. Dog breeding is extremely labour intensive work.
3. Can you afford the cost of such an exercise – stud fees, vet fees, feed, vaccinations, registration, advertising etc?
4. Do you have the temperament to breed dogs? The exercise can be very stressful and trying, particularly if you have little or no patience.
5. Can you be certain that you will be able to sell all of the puppies in the litter that you do not intend keeping?

If you can honestly manage to answer all of the above questions in the affirmative, then you are ready to embark on a long, stressful, but rewarding project.

Record keeping

To my mind, one of the most vital items that you must have for any breeding programme is a good record keeping system; by 'good', I mean accurate, up-to-date, efficient and effective. Such records are indispensable for fixing a desirable trait (or eliminating an undesirable trait), and for selecting suitable breeding stock. Using the records carefully, it is possible to select JRs that will produce good quality puppies, in looks, temperament and working ability. It is a sad but true fact that very few breeders of small animals keep any records at all, and the number that keep *good* records is almost non-existent.

For those readers breeding Parson Jack Russell terriers, a great deal of the record keeping is done by the Kennel Club. This is not to say, however, that the only records one should keep are those which refer to the breeding of the dog. Far from it. Records should refer to every aspect of your JR – its breeding, its temperament, working ability, markings, show successes, working days and so on. Never leave out anything from the records.

There are various methods which you can utilise, from notebooks to card indexes, loose-leaf pads to personal computers. Among my friends and associates, I am well known as a 'gadget man', but I will only continue to use such items if they really are useful to me. The most valuable asset that any of us possess is time; if by using a 'gadget' I can save myself some time, I feel that I should do so. With all new equipment and procedures, however, one must remember that there is always a learning curve – often quite steep – and so it will take time and effort before one is fully conversant with the equipment or procedure. Only when you are fully conversant with it will you begin to reap any benefits.

It is imperative, if you are to be successful in your breeding of JRs, that you maintain complete and accurate records from day one. These records can be kept in a card index, and/or in a book or some other central device. Whatever method you use, the record should contain the following information as a minimum:

name and/or reference number

breeder, if applicable

date of birth

parents, grandparents, and great grand parents

siblings

breeding/mating details (including sizes of litters)

shows entered, along with details of successes etc.

working ability

working awards

If using a card index, or notebook, all writing should be done using an indelible (waterproof) pen, since other inks will run when damp or when water is spilled on them. Never use pencil, as the writing will fade and you will have lost all of the information. Never trust to memory either, as it can fail all too often.

Not all of the above details need be written on the card, but all (and more) should be recorded in the 'stud book', a central record (not necessarily a book) of all details pertaining to your JRs. Without such a record, you will never be able to breed your animals successfully in an ordered and efficient manner. Neither will you be able to perpetuate any desirable trait, nor eliminate any undesirable ones.

The stud book

Many breeders use a loose-leaf folder for their stud book, and are quite happy with this arrangement. However, when using such books, it is very easy for a page to be lost, either through it falling out or simply because you forgot to replace it after removing it to copy the information. A hard-backed note book of A4 size is ideal, and you will have no trouble with pages going missing. Some breeders either enter the details of the females at one end of the book, and those of the males at the other end, or use two separate books. Others simply list their dogs one after another; I prefer to keep separate stud books for dogs and bitches.

A typical page in the stud book may be set out as follows:

KENNEL NAME   REFERENCE

HOUSE NAME

DATE OF BIRTH

BREEDER

PARENTS

PATERNAL G. PARENTS   MATERNAL G. PARENTS

PATERNAL G. G. PARENTS   MATERNAL G. G. PARENTS

SIBLINGS

NOTES

MATING AND BREEDING RECORD

Computers

Most households now have a personal computer (PC), and this can easily be used to store records. Indeed the main advantage with using PCs for record keeping is the ease with which relevant information can be retrieved and displayed. There are many software packages designed solely for use by dog breeders, and these are usually capable of printing out pedigrees for the progeny of any mating – a great time saver.

Computers may be in the form of desktop, laptop, notebook or even pocket-sized machines; the latter are often referred to as palmtops or organisers. I find that a palmtop, which can easily fit into a pocket, is extremely useful for recording details while one is actually with the dogs. With suitable software, this information can be 'uploaded' onto the PC back in the warmth of the home. Of course the PC itself is useless without the appropriate software, and so the choice of this software must be given thought. It is possible to use any database software, or even to write your own but, with so many good packages on the market at such an affordable price, I feel this is rather a waste of time.

For record keeping, some form of database is needed. This can, if the operator understands the system thoroughly, be very complicated and give many facilities which can prove invaluable. On the other hand, it is quite possible to buy software which is perfectly adequate, but which is user-friendly.

This type of software has a 'form making' facility, enabling the operator to design his own blank standard form (e.g. pedigree, breeding record etc.) The computer then stores both the blank and completed forms, enabling the operator to refer to records already written up (changing or adding to them if necessary), as well as displaying a blank form for completion if the operator wishes. It is also possible to programme the software to fill in these forms once the data on the two individuals is entered.

All records kept on computer have the advantage of being easily accessible, provided that some thought is given to their format, the fields chosen, and their storage. It is essential that you 'back up' your information after every use of the PC. Ideally, you should have the original data on one disk (usually the hard drive), a 'back up' copy, and a copy kept in a safe place other than the building in which the PC is stored. I have always been told that it is bad practice to store any data on the hard disk, as one fault can mean the loss of everything. There is also a risk that a hard disk will 'crash' and lose all of the information stored on it. While this is certainly not an everyday occurrence, thank goodness, it does occasionally happen and, if you have not backed up your files, then you will be in a sorry state. As stated earlier, if you are storing data on your hard disk, such a crash may cause you to lose all of the information that you have gathered over many years, and so backing up should be a regular habit, and carried out every time that you use your computer. I find that a dedicated back-up system, using either a tape or disk, is ideal, and my computer is programmed to prompt me to back up after every use.

Remember also to keep all floppy disks and other storage media away from sources of magnetism, since the information on them is stored by using magnetism, and external sources can corrupt the information, rendering it useless. Televisions, hi-fi speakers and video recorders are just some of the everyday items that are also powerful sources of magnetism.

Line-breeding and inbreeding

Inbreeding is the mating together of closely related animals, e.g. mother to son, father to daughter, brother to sister. There is a commonly held belief that inbreeding is highly undesirable, resulting in poor stock and small litters.

A young JR enthusiast proudly shows off his terrier . . .

LEFT AND OPPOSITE:

. . . while even not-so-young owners show the same pride in JRs.

This is not true. *Controlled* inbreeding is the method that has been used for countless generations to produce champion race horses, cattle, and dogs; records indicate that even the Parson used this method. If inbreeding was deleterious *per se*, then we would have no Syrian ('golden') hamsters in captivity, as the original stock, from which the vast majority of today's hamsters have descended, came from one female found in Syria in 1930. The only dangers with inbreeding occur when there is little or no control, or when not enough animals are available to allow selective breeding. Controlled inbreeding will fix good characteristics, and bring out others which are not readily apparent.

Line-breeding is a less acute form of inbreeding, in which more distantly related animals are mated, e.g. cousins, grandparents to grandchildren etc.

In practice, most breeders use a combination of the two methods, keeping their own animals and also using a stud dog from another breeder. This dog

may still be related, but distantly, and so the breeder is indulging in line-breeding. If the dog is completely unrelated, it is known as an 'outcross', as this is an animal that is entirely unrelated to its mate, and so will possess totally different genes; the introduction of unrelated blood is said to supply 'hybrid vigour'. According to some adherents of the theory, hybrid vigour will result in the offspring being tougher, more fertile, able to produce bigger and better litters, be less susceptible to illness and disease, and generally be fitter for survival. I feel that the idea has become overstated by many, and is not the panacea that some would have us believe.

The big danger with an outcross is that the animal could introduce genes which, although not showing any deleterious effect on that animal, when combined with the genes of other JRs could prove disastrous. Again *control* is needed in all breeding programmes, if success is to be achieved.

Selection of breeding stock

Many years ago, an old dog breeder told me about an old stockman's saying about breeding animals that is as true for JRs as it is for cows, horses, or any other type of animal; 'Put the best to the best, and hope for the best'. This adage should be borne in mind at all times when engaged in the breeding of your JRs.

For your breeding to be successful, you must start your programme with the best animals that you can obtain. If you do not own animals of the best calibre, then you should seriously consider buying young stock, rather than breed your own animals from mediocre stock since, to coin another adage, 'you will only get out what you put in'. In other words, poor stock bred with other poor stock will only produce more poor stock.

A half-way house between breeding your own JRs from your own stock and buying animals from another breeder is to utilise the services of a top grade dog (a stud) to mate with one of your bitches; the male in a mating is known as the 'sire', while the female is known as the 'dam'. Your bitch must, of course, be of a high standard, or you will simply be wasting your time. You will have to pay for the stud services of the male; this payment can be made in cash, but is often the 'pick of the litter'. Unfortunately, if the supplier of the stud wishes to obtain good stock (just as you do), he will almost certainly choose the best of the litter, leaving you with the rest, which may or may not contain a puppy or puppies of the correct standard for you.

If you do not know whether the animals that you possess are good, bad or indifferent, then you should ask an experienced breeder for his opinion and, if you are breeding for show, attend as many shows as possible to get a feel for the standard. If you are showing your JRs, you should firstly carefully read the standards set out by the various club(s) of your choice, and compare your

JR(s) to these standards. However, it has to be said that reading about a subject is not as good as having first hand experience of it. Attendance at a show will give you the opportunity of talking to experienced breeder/exhibitors about your stock and what makes a good show JR. Remember that different clubs and different judges will interpret the standards slightly differently from each other, and so you should try to visit shows in other areas, rather than merely staying in your own locale.

The stud dog

It is important to choose the sire of your next generation of JRs with great care. Do not rush to take the easy option and simply borrow the services of the nearest dog. Some 50% of the sire's genetic material will be passed to every puppy, so you must ensure that the sire is the right one for the job.

If you intend breeding a litter for show purposes, the stud dog must have gained regular success on the show bench, and thus possess very few faults in his conformation. However, do not overlook temperament. To me, and I feel to any who truly have the interests of the breed at heart, temperament is as important as any other trait, if not more so than many. If a dog has a wonderful conformation but limited intelligence and poor temperament, I do not use his services. It is better to seek out a near relative – brother, cousin etc. – and utilise him for the mating. Very often, such a mating seems to produce better progeny than using the champion himself.

As well as having the necessary certificates and other such paperwork, the stud dog should have both testes descended, and not be too fat. He should be well-muscled and active, and not have been overworked in his stud duties. The latter may well result in a low sperm count, with all of its related problems.

Carefully examine the dog's pedigree, and look for similar ancestors to those of the bitch, appearing three or four generations back.

The brood bitch

It is arguable that the brood bitch is the most important part of the breeding project. This bitch must be able to produce good litters which grow well and also conform to the standards of the show ring and/or the working require-ments of a hunting JR. The bitch's pedigree is obviously a good place to start when searching for suitability. It is not essential that the bitch has actually excelled in the ring or the working arena, but she should be fit and sound, of good conformation, active and intelligent. The temperament of all breeding dogs should be good, but that of brood bitches must be excellent. They must also be easy whelpers and excellent mothers. The bitch in any mating will obviously contribute 50% of the genes of the new generation, and she is also the manufacturer of the puppies and their food supply for the first few weeks of their life.

Any bitch used for breeding must be fully grown before the mating, in at least her second oestrus or heat; if possible, I like to leave my bitches until they are in their third heat. Before she comes into season, the bitch must be given regular exercise and a balanced diet, ensuring that, by the time she is ready for mating, she is lean and active. Overweight and lethargic bitches do not make good mothers. Worming should be carried out a few weeks before the actual mating, and this should be repeated every two weeks during pregnancy and throughout lactation. Do not use anthelmintics (wormers) obtained from a pet shop; go to your veterinary surgeon, who will recommend and supply the best type and quantities needed. All vaccinations must be up-to-date before the bitch is mated.

After the mating, it is possible for an experienced breeder or (preferably) the vet, to test for pregnancy by palpating the bitch to feel for the pups, at about the 22nd day of pregnancy. At this stage, the embryos appear to be like a string of beads. Around the 30th day, these embryos become surrounded by fluid, making it extremely difficult to diagnose pregnancy until the 5th or 6th week. Many veterinary surgeons now offer an ultra sound (scanning) service.

Not everyone's ideal of a Jack Russell! Many small brown or black-and-white terriers are erroneously described and sold as JRs to unsuspecting people.

A word of caution; even where embryos are found at this stage, they may not result in the birth of any puppies, since they can be completely absorbed by the bitch before reaching full term.

The bitch's diet

For at least four weeks prior to mating, the dam's diet should have been given special attention. I find it best to give a mixed diet of complete feed, meat and biscuits. According to research carried out at the University of Chicago, USA, feeding the bitch a diet containing up to 4% extra fat is extremely beneficial for both the bitch and her puppies. The researchers claim that such a diet will give the bitch better reproduction rates, and also that the puppies from such a bitch will have a higher weight gain than those from litters where the dam has not been given this fat.

As detailed in the chapter on feeding, extra calcium will also be required, as well as extra protein, during pregnancy and lactation. The quantities of food will need to be increased also; this is covered later in this chapter.

Fertility

Many things can affect the fertility of both the bitch and the stud dog, and there are yet more considerations to be made when preparing to breed from your JRs.

Dogs are, to a degree, photoperiodic, that is to say, their biological clock is regulated by the ratio of daylight to darkness. Their fertility is greatest between the months of April and August. Stud dogs which have been over-worked will have a lower sperm count than normal, although a proper diet can help reduce this problem. Diet can affect the fertility of both dog and bitch, and the addition of green vegetables to the diet of both dog and bitch will prove beneficial.

Pre-mating planning and checks

Well before the mating is due, but after you have selected a short list of possible stud dogs for your brood bitch, you should start making plans and checking on the suitability of the members of that list. Are all the stud candidates tested and clear of all hereditary diseases?

The mating

There are various theories about when to have a bitch mated, in order that there is the best possible chance of her being made pregnant. Before looking at those theories, we need to have a basic understanding of oestrus in a bitch.

Canine species, like most other animals, can only mate when they are 'in season' or 'on heat'. Although most lay people take this as meaning the same as 'being in oestrus', there is a difference. Bitches are mono-oestrous, meaning that, unlike most other mammals, they only have one oestrus during each breeding season. As far as we know, this is unique in the animal kingdom. This phenomenon obviously limits the opportunities for the bitch to mate and conceive.

The bitch's cycle can be divided into four phases, although these should not be seen as separate entities, as they merge into each other. The phases are – pro-oestrus, oestrus, met-oestrus and anoestrus.

Pro-oestrus
With an average duration of nine days, this is the beginning of heat in the bitch. The vulva swells, and there is a bloodstained discharge. Dogs will be very attracted by the bitch at this stage, but she will not allow them to mate with her.

Oestrus
Lasting about nine days, this is the period when the bitch will accept a mating from a dog (any dog). The vulva is extremely enlarged and swollen, and the discharge is now 'straw coloured'. About two days after oestrus begins, ovulation occurs.

Met-oestrus
This stage, which can last as long as ninety days, occurs only in the unmated bitch. This is when an unmated bitch may show signs of a phantom pregnancy.

Anoestrus
This is the period between cycles, and determines how often the bitch will come into season.

In JRs, most females reach puberty at about six to seven months, but some may not experience their first season until they are much older. If a bitch has not had a season by the time she is two years old, then veterinary advice must be sought.

Some breeders recommend, and themselves strictly adhere to, having the bitch mated on the 14th day of oestrus. Others recommend that the bitch is mated when the discharge changes colour, while still others will leave a dog running with the bitch throughout the heat.

Veterinary surgeons can now help us determine the best days on which to have the bitch mated, i.e. those days when she is most likely to conceive. This is done by measuring the hormone levels of the bitch to be mated, which allows the vet to inform the breeder when ovulation is about to occur, or has just occurred. The breeder is then able to take the bitch to the stud dog during her peak of fertility. This is achieved by taking a simple blood sample.

Where the bitch has successfully bred in the past, only one sample, taken between ten and eleven days after the onset of heat, will be necessary. In this case, it is highly likely that the bitch will need to be mated in one or two days, usually two.

In other bitches, particularly those that have been mated but have not conceived, the manufacturers of the testing kit recommend that the first sample should be taken at seven days after the onset of pro-oestrus, and then every two to three days thereafter, until such time as the test indicates optimum fertility.

Although there are other methods utilised by some veterinary surgeons to determine the optimum mating time for a bitch, notably vaginal cytology (which involves a smear being taken from the bitch in question) and vaginoscopy (where the veterinary surgeon will need to examine the lining of the bitch's vagina using a vaginoscope), I feel that the best and most reliable results are obtained from the measurement of hormone levels.

It is worth taking the time and trouble to have your bitch tested, as this can save much money, time and effort, as you will know for certain that the bitch is being mated at the optimum time, and so should have the best possible chance of conceiving. As taking a bitch to a stud dog often involves much travel and often an overnight stay, the advantages are obvious.

Whichever method you use for determining the time for your bitch to be mated, it is recommended that two matings, 48 hours apart, are the absolute minimum in order to ensure success.

Once all has been arranged, take your bitch to the stud dog owner's kennels in plenty of time, so that you do not have to rush, throwing the bitch around in the car in the process. On the way there, close to but not at the stud kennels, give your bitch the chance to urinate. Remember that she is at her optimum fertility and acceptability for ANY dog, and so she should be walked on a lead, with you keeping a very strict vigil for any dogs in the vicinity.

Once you arrive at the kennels, you should leave your bitch in the car, preferably in the security of a dog cage in the back of the car, while you speak to the owner of the stud dog and ascertain how the owner wants the process to proceed. Once this is settled, you should put your bitch on her lead, and take her out of the car, walking her to the designated spot. At this point, it is best if both dog and bitch are taken off their leads and allowed to run and play together. This may last for several minutes until the dog mounts the bitch. As he does so, he will penetrate the bitch's vulva with his penis, clasping the bitch around the waist with his front paws.

If you suspect that your bitch may be snappy, she should be fitted with a muzzle. Indeed, some owners of stud dogs will insist on this, in order to eliminate any risk of injury to their dog.

Once he has mounted her, the dog will give several strong thrusts, and then will 'tie' with the bitch. The dog's penis will remain inside the bitch, although the dog will climb off the bitch's back. At this stage, it is usual for the dog and bitch to stand facing in opposite directions. The tie will last for anything from five minutes to an hour (the average time is twenty minutes), and during this time, the owners should keep both dog and bitch steady. It is at this time that some bitches will become snappy. There is no need to try to break the tie; to do so would be dangerous. The tie will break spontaneously.

Throughout the whole mating procedure, the owner of the stud dog is in complete command, and their instructions should be obeyed without question.

Once the mating is concluded, the bitch should be walked back to her cage in the car, and then, while she settles down, you can carry out the administrative duties. The stud fee must be paid in full at the time of the first mating, and on payment, you should be given a signed pedigree of the stud dog and, if the terrier is a Parson Jack Russell, a Kennel Club form signed by the stud owner. This form will certify that the mating took place, giving the date, and is necessary for you to register the litter when it arrives. If your bitch is Kennel Club registered (i.e. a PJRT), then you should also check the pedigree of the stud dog to ensure that it contains the dog's Kennel Club registration number.

Once the bitch has been mated on the agreed number of occasions, it is time to take her home, always remembering that your bitch is still receptive to dogs and at her peak of fertility. You do not want any mistakes at this stage.

It is worth noting that a long-standing 'arrangement' has been that, if the bitch does not deliver a litter, then the owner of the stud dog used will allow her to have a free mating on her next season. It is always worth asking if this is the case *before* the mating arrangements are made.

The birth of the litter

Although many breeders and, indeed, authors, will state that the bitch's gestation period (pregnancy) is 63 days, it can, in fact, last between 54 and 72 days, with the average being 60 days. This is the actual time between fertilisation and whelping. Therefore, if a bitch ovulates early in that particular season, she will already have eggs waiting to be fertilised on the actual day of mating. On the other hand, some bitches are quite slow to ovulate, and this will result in a seemingly long pregnancy.

To allow for this variation in length of pregnancy, the breeder must be ready, with all preparations made, and everything in place, for the bitch to whelp at any time from eight weeks after the actual mating.

During the pregnancy, you must be careful to keep up the good diet, but do not add vitamin and mineral supplements unless under the direct supervision and instructions of a qualified veterinary surgeon. To ignore this advice is to risk both litter and dam.

Ensure that the bitch is treated for any ecto-parasites, such as fleas and lice, and also wormed, again in accordance with veterinary advice. Do not allow her to become obese, and give her regular bouts of exercise, reducing their duration as whelping day approaches. While out exercising the bitch, prevent her from going down rabbit burrows or fox dens. It is quite possible that, with

A young handler and his puppy come under the scrutiny of the judge at a JRTCGB show.

81

her increased girth, she may become stuck. Of course, keeping any Jack Russell from investigating such subterranean places is likely to prove a difficult task, but it must be done. It is best to not let your pregnant bitch venture down any such holes, purely on the ground of her safety.

During the bitch's pregnancy, she may well start to dig. In the wild, this 'cave' would become her den, where she would whelp. This is not necessarily harmful, and although many people believe that, as it is natural, it would be harmful to prevent her doing this, such digging bouts should be limited. This is particularly true where the bitch is digging in sandy soil, because of the ever-present hazard of possible earth falls, which could trap and seriously harm the bitch.

Preparations

Well before the 'due date', thought must be given to the actual whelping, and a whelping room prepared. This could be the bitch's kennel, a room in the human home, or a shed in the garden. The room should be fairly isolated from the human family, and also from other animals, and have a heater and a fan. You should also have a good supply of water, preferably both hot and cold. If the room does not have its own hot water tap, a large electric kettle is an excellent way of getting hot water when you need it.

A telephone in the room can be a great asset, especially if things go wrong, and you need to contact the vet. Cordless or mobile phones are probably the best options, as either will allow you to move around while having any necessary telephone conversations with the vet.

Whichever room you choose, ensure that preparations are completed well before the expected date of the bitch's whelping.

Large amounts of newspaper are essential, and the breeder would be wise to begin stockpiling these as soon as the bitch has been mated. Keep only clean newspapers. Many newsagents, or even the newspaper publishers, will be happy to let you have quite large quantities of unsold newspapers. Friends and family can also be prevailed upon to supply their newspapers, once the family have finished with them. Remember, you will need a lot of newspapers in the first few days of the life of the puppies, and it is virtually impossible to have too many.

I like to place a fairly comfortable chair in the whelping room, as I know that I may be in there for quite some time, once the action starts. Some breeders install a camp bed and sleeping bag, feeling they need to be next to the bitch in the last few days before whelping, in case she starts early. Although this is laudable, I find it impractical, as I have lots of other work to do, and feel that the rest I would get in my own bed is the best preparation for this. I prefer to have some kind of monitor in the whelping room. Until very recently, this was an 'intercom'; this was switched so that I could hear every noise that the bitch made, and the receiver was carried by me wherever I went, and placed beside my bed at night. I have now added to this by installing a closed circuit television camera. Although this may sound very grand, the price for the system, which utilises a small TV for the screen, was remarkably affordable. I can now keep an eye on the bitch in the whelping room at any time, even when I am a considerable distance from the room itself.

Other items which I like to have in the whelping room are an angle poise lamp, a small cardboard box, complete with a hot water bottle wrapped in an old towel, into which the individual puppies will be placed while they are drying out, a sturdy table (for possible veterinary examination of the puppies or dam), the whelping box and my 'whelping kit'.

This kit consists of items which I feel will be useful, based on previous experiences with whelping. The contents include the following;

- A pair of surgeon's latex, disposable gloves
- A tube of KY jelly
- An electronic thermometer
- A litre of glucose mixture (one tablespoon per litre of water), along with spare glucose powder
- A box of strong tissues
- A couple of old towels or ripped up sheets
- Two or three large plastic refuse bags
- A torch which fits on my head
- Electronic scales
- Notebook and pen
- Nail brush, anti-bacterial soap and a towel (for myself)
- A pair of good scissors
- A small container of antiseptic solution
- Coffee-making kit *
- A good novel to read *
- A Walkman *

Written in large bold indelible ink on the top of the box containing this kit are the telephone numbers of my veterinary surgeon – just in case.

The whelping box

The old-fashioned design of a whelping box was an open-topped box, with bars running down each side, about 20 cm from and parallel with each side. Many breeders are happy to use such a device, and I am sure that these

* after all, whelping can take a long time!

whelping boxes have served their owners well. However, after recently reading several articles and books on the subject, I used a different design for our latest litter. Using two very strong cardboard boxes, which I obtained from a local computer retailer, I made a bed for the bitch with a cover over, very much resembling a cave. The bitch in question, Scilla, loved it and settled in almost immediately.

I cut several pieces of 'Vetbed' to fit the bottom of the bed, but keep them until well after the whelping.

I also place an electric heater pad in one corner of the whelping box.

The whelping

The time it can take for a bitch to deliver her litter can vary enormously, from one hour to almost forty-eight hours. Most of the litters which our bitches have whelped have been delivered in less than twelve hours, with an average of eight hours, and the vast majority without any complications whatsoever.

Many breeders do not wish to risk being taken by surprise, and so will take the bitch's temperature two or three times each day from just before the expected whelping date. It is a well-known fact that the bitch's temperature will drop about 24 hours before she whelps. The normal temperature of an adult JR is 38.6°C (101.5°F), and this may fall to as low as 36.1°C (97°F). It should be noted that normally, the bitch's temperature is lower (about 1°C) in the last week of pregnancy, and this should be taken into account when making any calculations about drops in temperature of the bitch.

In the early stages of whelping, the bitch will appear restless and refuse food; this may happen from 18 to 24 hours prior to whelping. She may have long (up to 24 hours) periods of panting, which lead to only intermittent sleep. Give your bitch, at this stage, a couple of newspapers to shred, which she will do as a reaction to the pain of whelping. Just before birth, it is natural to see large amounts of stringy-looking mucus come out of the bitch's vagina.

The bitch will stop panting, and seem very calm and quiet, and she will be seen to be having contractions, pushing the pups to her rear end. Just before the first puppy appears, the bitch will expel the amniotic sac (the 'water bag'), which is black in appearance. Sometimes, this sac ruptures high in the vagina, and all the breeder will see is a gush of fluid. Shortly after this sac appears, the puppy will come out, usually (but certainly not always) head first. Once the puppy is out, be prepared to help the bitch open the caul (the membrane cover or sac covering the newborn puppy). This is particularly important with a bitch's first litter, as she may well not know what to do. If this is the case, once the puppy has been freed from the sac, he should be rubbed dry with a towel; vigorous rubbing will help him get breathing. Then, using your fingers, push the blood in the umbilicus towards the puppy and, using sterilised scissors, cut the cord as far away from the puppy as possible. Next, place the puppy on one of the bitch's nipples, to take his first feed. It is important for the welfare of both puppy and dam that the puppy and dam are allowed to bond as soon as possible after the birth.

The afterbirth, or placenta, is often expelled by the bitch at the same time as, or just after, the first puppy. The bitch should be allowed to eat as many of these placentas, which will follow each puppy, as she wishes.

In between puppies, clean the whelping area, and replace the soiled newspaper with fresh, putting the soiled papers in a sack for later incineration.

Stay with the bitch throughout the whelping, and only interfere if there is a real need; let her do as much as she can on her own. If in any doubt about how the whelping is proceeding, contact your veterinary surgeon immediately. Allow the bitch to drink the glucose mixture, mentioned earlier, at frequent intervals throughout the whelping. If there is any chill in the air, use the heater; conversely, if it is too warm, use the fan.

An examination by a qualified veterinary surgeon, of both the dam and the pups, should be organised within 48 hours after the whelping. The vet will be looking for the bitch's uterus to be empty and contracting in size. He will also check for any signs of infection, and probably give the bitch a shot of the hormone oxytocin. This will help ensure that the uterus contracts properly, and expels all of its contents

A greenish discharge, known as the lochia, will be visible coming from the bitch's vagina for about 24 hours after the whelping. This is followed by a dark brown blood discharge, which will persist for several weeks.

Normally, JRs are easy whelpers, and seem to experience very few complications. Litters are usually of four to six puppies, each one weighing between 115 and 250 gm (4 and 8 oz) at birth. They are born with the same coloration that they will have as adults, unlike some breeds.

Possible problems

If your bitch has gone for more than two to two and a half hours between puppies, and has still not delivered, despite her having contractions, it is likely that there is a problem, and so you should consult the veterinary surgeon. Try not to panic, but give the vet the facts about the process to date. You should have been recording the times that each puppy was born; I also weigh each one immediately after birth. The vet will advise you on your next course of action.

Known as dystocia, the inability to whelp is unusual in Jack Russell terriers, but is not unknown. It is thought that the affliction may be genetically inherited, but there are other causes. These include the first time breeding from a bitch over five years of age, a slackness in the bitch's muscles, obesity, a general lack of fitness, or even a uterus that has been overstretched because of the number and/or size of puppies carried. Sometimes, sheer fatigue prevents the bitch from expelling her puppies. Whatever the cause, veterinary treatment is necessary, and should be sought at once.

If the puppy does not breathe straight away after birth, rub him vigorously with a towel, which should get him breathing. If this does not work, pick him up by the hindlegs (one hand on each leg, just above the knee joint) and, with your arms straight, swing him from side to side from about the four o'clock position to the eight o'clock position. This transfers the weight of the puppy's organs onto and off the diaphragm, which alters the pressure in the lungs, pulling air in and then expelling it. Swing the puppy about four or six times, and then check for breathing, giving the puppy a vigorous rub if he is still not breathing. Unless you are very experienced, it is unwise to try to give a Jack Russell puppy mouth to mouth respiration, although if doing so you should use a small bore tube, such as the empty barrel of a ball point pen. Use a finger over the hole on the side of the barrel to regulate the pressure, breathe gently, every two or three seconds, and watch the puppy's chest for expansion. Too much pressure can cause severe damage to the puppy's lungs.

Where a large proportion of the litter are dead at birth, this would indicate some type of infection, such as distemper, hepatitis or leptospirosis. If post-mortem examination of the cadavers reveals this to be the case, the infection must be completely cured before any more mating with the bitch is even considered. All other animals (including the stud dog) who have been in contact with the bitch should also be examined and, where relevant, treated accordingly.

I recommend that all puppies that are dead at birth are given a post-mortem examination by a qualified veterinary surgeon, and the findings acted upon.

The mouth of the puppy should be examined for cleft palate, where the two halves of the hard palate in the roof of the mouth have failed to join and fuse together. A sure indication that the puppy has a cleft palate is when milk can be seen, while the puppy is feeding, running down the puppy's nose. Such a puppy will never be fit and healthy, and euthanasia is the best solution for all puppies showing this affliction.

A 'lump' seen near the umbilicus could indicate an umbilical hernia. Small umbilical hernias may well heal themselves, but larger ones will need veterinary attention. Such a lump in the groin area of a puppy may well indicate an inguinal hernia, where part of the abdominal contents or an abdominal organ protrude through the inguinal canal in the puppy's groin. Veterinary treatment should be sought.

The Jack Russell's jaw should be a scissor bite. Where the upper jaw protrudes beyond the lower, this is known as 'overshot', and where the lower jaw protrudes beyond the upper, this is known as 'undershot'. Both conditions may be hereditary, and will severely affect the chances of a show dog. Unless the affliction is severe, it should not affect the working terrier nor the pet terrier, but no dog showing such a detrimental abnormality should be bred from.

Post-whelping care of the bitch

Just after she has completed the whelping, the bitch should be offered a meal of chicken or fish or some other easily digested food. Once she has eaten this, put her on a lead, and give her a ten to fifteen minute walk, well away from any other dogs. This is something that you may well have to do every day for the next week or so, as the bitch will not want to leave her new litter. This can lead to her forgetting everything she was taught regarding toilet training, and so the walks – two or three times each day – will be essential. These walks also give her the opportunity to relax a little, as raising up to six puppies can be very demanding work for the bitch.

To allow for her reluctance to leave the new litter, you should, quite literally feed the bitch in her bed, by placing meals very close to the bed, allowing her to eat without leaving the litter. The water bowl, too, should be placed next to the bed. I never give my bitches milk, especially at a time like this, as milk tends to scour (cause diarrhoea). This will obviously lead to dehydration, and the results could be dire for both the dam and the puppies concerned. Far better to simply give her normal water, to help replenish the fluid which she will lose every time the puppies suckle on her teats. Change the newspaper for Vetbed, immediately after the whelping, and this, too must be replaced by fresh material at regular intervals. By having several (I recommend three to four) pieces of Vetbed, this will allow you to wash some while others are in use, and always have at least one spare piece, for any accidents that the bitch may have.

Until the puppies are between 19 and 21 days of age, the bitch will lick their rear ends, thus stimulating them to urinate and defecate. The dam will consume these waste materials. The bitch should be groomed and kept clean in general throughout the period she is with the litter.

She should receive regular daily exercise (two or three times each day as an absolute minimum), and her diet should be adjusted according to her requirements (see chapter 4 on feeding). To allow for the extra drain on her physical resources that rearing a litter of puppies will entail, her feeds should be more regular and the amounts increased on an almost daily basis. Lactation is very demanding for the bitch, and it is not unusual for a lactating bitch to require more than four times the energy input that she needed during her 'normal' life. Consequently, the amounts needed are very large, and so need to be split into six or eight meals in each 24-hour period. With such large amounts of food being eaten, the amounts of water consumed will also increase at a similar rate. Under no circumstances must a lactating bitch be left without water at any time.

Do not supplement the diet with extra vitamins and minerals without the express instruction of a qualified veterinary surgeon.

Weaning the new puppies

Weaning, the changing of a puppy's diet from liquid (i.e. bitch's milk) to solids, is a very stressful time for the puppies, and usually begins at about two to three weeks of age, to be completed by the time the puppies are six or seven weeks old.

Today, it is very easy to buy and feed proprietary brands of puppy food, where the material is easy to chew and digest and, of course, contains all of the necessary nutrients vital if the puppies are to grow into strong, healthy adult terriers. Trying to cut corners and feed a cheap second rate diet to puppies at this stage will have catastrophic results in the future. This is a time to lay down firm foundations on which the JR can build.

It is vital that, throughout puppyhood, a strict hygiene regime is followed, as puppies are extremely sensitive and susceptible to bacterial infections, all too readily passed to them via dirty feed and water dishes. Wash and scrub all dishes and cutlery etc. used thoroughly in a top quality disinfectant, such as Trigene, ensuring that all residues are rinsed off well before the dishes are given to the puppies. The dishes used must be shallow and wide, enabling the puppies to reach into the dish. Unfortunately, this also allows them to bodily climb into the dish, and often urinate and defecate in the dish, hence the hygiene routine must be 100% effective.

In the early stages, I encourage the puppies to eat the food by gently dipping their muzzles in the feed. The puppies' natural instinct is then to lick it off and – Hey Presto! They are eating. Several feeds should be given to the puppies each day, although they will, of course, still depend largely on the bitch's milk. I like to ensure that the litter is given an assortment of flavours at this stage, as I find this helps them to accept a wide range of feeds in later life.

When the litter is about three weeks old, I take the bitch away from them for longer and more frequent intervals, during which they are fed and given a dish of bitch milk substitute, such as Lactol. This action both allows the bitch's milk to dry up, and encourages the puppies to find an alternative source of nutrition.

By the time they are six or seven weeks of age, the puppies should be completely weaned from the bitch, and her milk supply totally dried up. If the bitch still has milk at this stage, veterinary advice should be sought and acted upon.

Do not forget that, once weaning is over, the bitch's daily food intake must be adjusted back to what it was before she was mated. If her weight has altered drastically, then a diet may be called for, but, again, veterinary advice must be sought before the breeder embarks on any course of action aimed at adjusting this difference.

Feeding the puppies

Almost every dog breeder to whom I have ever spoken has a different feeding regime for his puppies; most seem to work very well indeed. However, two guiding tenets must be adhered to by all breeders if strong, healthy pups are going to result.

1. Large amounts of food must be eaten by the puppies, as they require nutrients for growth and maintenance. Weight for weight, puppies will, therefore, require far more feed than an adult dog of the same breed.

2. Because of the size of their stomachs (small), they will require to be fed little, and very often.

At about eight weeks of age, puppies should be fed at least four meals each day; the number of meals should be progressively reduced as the puppies grow older. By the time they are 24 weeks, they should be on two meals each day. The frequency of these meals should also be divided throughout the day. For example at four meals, a puppy should be fed at 8 a.m., 12 noon, 4 p.m. and the last meal at 8 p.m.

Whatever is fed, it should be concentrated, thereby reducing the sheer bulk, and also balanced for a puppy. As discussed in chapter 4, a puppy's dietary requirements are very much different from those of an adult JR. Once you have selected an appropriate diet, this should not be changed abruptly, as this will result in dietary diarrhoea, and all the risks associated with that affliction. Neither should you, in an attempt to do the best by your puppies, feed vitamin and mineral supplements. Obviously, if you are feeding a complete balanced diet, the addition of any supplement will put it out of balance. At best, this is unnecessary, at worst it could be downright dangerous.

Development of the puppies

Puppies are born with a covering of fur; in the Jack Russell, this fur remains the same colour throughout the life of the dog. Their eyes and ears are sealed at birth, with their eyes opening at between seven and ten days. By about two weeks, the puppy can see, although his sight will not be equal to that of an adult until he is about one month old. Their ears open at about two weeks, and their hearing is acute by about seven weeks. The puppies' first teeth will appear between two and three weeks of age, and they will be able to eat from a dish at about three and a half weeks.

By three weeks of age, there is no need for the bitch to stimulate the puppies to urinate and defecate, and within five days of this time, they will be able to stand and balance while they do their toileting. Siblings will start to play among themselves at about four weeks, at which time they can walk and run. Playing with toys will begin at about seven weeks, and by six weeks the litter will start to establish its own hierarchical structure, manifesting itself in the play of the puppies.

CHAPTER 6

SHOWING

For many owners of Jack Russells, showing is their *raison d'être*. To complicate matters in the Jack Russell show world, there are two camps, with different standards and ideas. As I have already stated, I do not intend to get into the debate about which is best, or which standard is nearer to the terrier bred by the Parson himself. The following is an introduction to the show or exhibition of Jack Russell terriers, and showing in general. Where appropriate, I have given specifics of one standard or another, but this is in no way intended to imply acceptance or otherwise of that standard or club.

The results board at Cruft's.

Principles of dog shows

The first dog show ever held was on 28–29 June 1859, at the Town Hall, Newcastle upon Tyne, organised by Messrs Shorthose and Pape. Entries were limited to pointers and setters, and there were sixty entries with three judges for each breed. Some of the judges of one class had entries in other classes – not a state of affairs that would be allowed today.

The show was a huge success, and led to the formation of the Birmingham Dog Show Society, and a show for 'sporting dogs' later that year. Since then, of course, many more dog societies and dog shows have been established and, it has to be admitted, some of these have ceased to exist. Today, the dog-showing world is a thriving industry, with countless clubs and societies all around the world, all of whom organise one or more shows each year.

Much more recently, in fact in 1976, the Jack Russell Terrier Club of Great Britain was formed and 1983 saw the formation of the Parson Jack Russell Terrier Club. It was the PJRTC which fought and eventually won, the battle for Kennel Club recognition of the breed. Although these two bodies do not see eye to eye, both are actively encouraging what they see as the best interests of the dog we know and love so well, the Jack Russell terrier.

To those not involved in showing dogs, dog shows and the act of showing, are much misunderstood. I once heard a regular exhibitor at a dog show sum up the Fancy as 'a quest for perfection and excellence', and I feel that this paints the picture well. Of course, many people would argue about the 'perfection' for which those of us who breed and show dogs strive, but strive we still do.

In each litter which we produce, we look for that 'perfect' puppy, and use as our blue print the standards set down by the club to which we belong. Whenever a new litter arrives, I am sure that many breeders will feel that the Sporting Parson is casting his critical gaze upon them from the gates of Heaven.

Dog shows

If you are keeping Parson Jack Russell terriers, and your JR is Kennel Club registered, you will probably wish to enter your dog at a Kennel Club recognised show. There are several different types of show, and I will try to explain their differences and the criteria applied to entries for that show.

What showing is all about. A proud owner displays both JR and the winner's rosette.

The Kennel Club allows the following types of show to be organised under its aegis:

- Exemption shows
- Matches
- Primary shows
- Sanction shows
- Limited shows
- Open shows
- Championship shows

Exemption shows

Both registered and unregistered dogs are allowed to enter exemption shows, with up to five classes for pedigree dogs (whether the dogs are registered or not), and an unlimited number of classes for dogs which are pedigree or not, registered or not. If you have a pedigree JR (whether or not it is registered), at an exemption show, you will be able to enter it into the 'Any Variety Terriers' class.

No puppy under six months can be entered in a Kennel Club exemption show, or in any other show organised under the auspices of the Kennel Club.

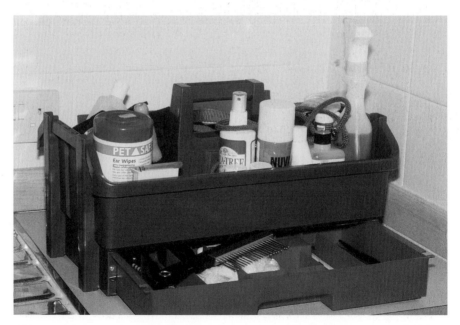

A kit containing grooming and other equipment is essential for the adequate care of all dogs.

A Jack Russell Club of Great Britain show taking place at a country fair in England.

Exemption shows are really to try to encourage the newcomers to the Fancy, and so dogs which have won the awards listed below cannot be entered into any classes at an exemption show.

- Challenge certificate
- Reserve challenge certificate
- Junior warrant

Obedience classes may be held at an exemption dog show, but all classes in obedience must be different from those set by the Kennel Club in their 'Rules and Regulations'. No dog can be entered in any of these obedience classes, where that dog has won an Obedience Certificate.

In conjunction with the Exemption Dog Show, and under a separate licence from the Kennel Club, a KC recognised club or society may organise an agility test, but not stage any courses for agility or obstacles. Under these circumstances, the course must be run in accordance with KC 'Regulations for Agility Tests'.

The cash prizes offered at most dog shows are very small, and at Exemption Dog Shows, must not exceed £100.

Matches

Matches are organised between clubs and societies, or within a single club or society. They involve competition by elimination, on a one-to-one basis, and

Both bicoloured and tricoloured JRs are recognised markings.

any club or society can hold up to twelve matches every year. If the club or society has any 'branches', each one of these is allowed to hold one match every calendar month, if they so wish.

A maximum of sixty-four dogs are allowed to compete at any one match, and all of these must be the property of members of those clubs involved.

Primary shows

Only full members of the club or society staging a primary show may enter dogs in the classes at that show, and entry is also limited to dogs which have never won a first prize at any show, other than in a puppy, special puppy, minor puppy and special minor puppy class. Likewise, dogs which have won a challenge certificate, or a reserve challenge certificate, are also excluded from entry to any class at a primary show.

On days other than weekends and bank holidays, primary shows cannot start before 5 p.m., although at weekends and on bank holidays, they can commence at 2 p.m.

Entries can be taken on the day of the show.

Sanction shows, Limited shows, Open shows and Champion shows

For all of these shows, proper benching must be provided by the show organisers, and the number of show rings, which each have to be at least 6 ½ metres (20 feet) wide and contain free floor space of at least 56 square metres (200 square feet), must be appropriate to the numbers and breeds of dog. Every ring has to be enclosed, either by seats or in some other way. In outside shows, as well as the rings intended for use on that day, there have to be others under cover.

All judges have to be provided with measures (and weighing scales for those breeds or classes subject to any type of weight limit) to help them carry out their judging duties. Organisers must provide areas for the owners of the exhibits to groom their dogs, if the owners so wish, and there have to be clearly defined exercise areas. The organisers also have to provide space for cages and trolleys to be stored by the owners.

Veterinary support

All organisers of these types of show also have to ensure that there is adequate veterinary support, i.e. that a qualified and registered veterinary surgeon is available throughout the show. The vet must also be given access to a suitable place where he/she can examine any dogs necessary. Finally, there has to be a place where any dog suspected of carrying an infectious or contagious disease can be kept for the remainder of the show.

Classes

In single-breed shows, there must be a minimum of twelve classes, including the mandatory Open Class. If the show caters for more than one breed, there must be a minimum of sixteen classes, including an Open Class for each breed. Some shows are organised on 'Group' lines, and these must have an Any Variety Not Separately Classified class, unless the show has a class for every breed eligible for classification.

Awards

In every class, there must be at least four awards – First, Second, Third and Reserve, and printed awards must be given. For classes for a single breed, a Best of Breed award must be given.

There are many other rules, but the above will help the reader judge just how much organisation goes into any show. Although these rules and regulations are from the Kennel Club, shows run outside the Kennel Club framework will carry similar rules and regulations.

In addition, there are agility, obedience and working tests, trials and shows which you may wish to enter your JR in. Contact your club secretary or the secretary of specialist clubs which conduct these events.

Waiting for the judge can be such tiring work!

The Jack Russell Terrier Club of Great Britain's standard for the Jack Russell terrier

CHARACTERISTICS –The terrier must present a lively, active and alert appearance. It should impress with its fearless and happy disposition. It should be remembered that the Jack Russell is a working terrier, and should retain these instincts. Nervousness, cowardice and over-aggression should be discouraged, and the dog should always appear confident.

GENERAL APPEARANCE – A sturdy, tough terrier, very much on its toes all the time, measuring between 25 cm (10 in) and 37 cm (15 in) at the withers. The body length must be in proportion to the height, and it should present a compact, balanced image, always being in solid, hard condition.

HEAD – Should be well balanced and in proportion to the body. The skull should be flat, of moderate width at the ears, narrowing to the eyes. There should be a defined stop, but not over-pronounced. The length of the muzzle from the nose to the stop should be slightly shorter than the distance from the stop to the occiput. The nose should be black. The jaw should be powerful and well-boned with strongly muscled cheeks.

EYES – Should be almond-shaped, dark in colour, and full of life and intelligence.

EARS – Small 'V'-shaped, drop-ears carried forward close to the head and of moderate thickness.

MOUTH – Strong teeth with the upper set slightly overlapping the lower.

NECK – Clean and muscular, of good length, gradually widening at the shoulders.

FOREQUARTERS – The shoulders should be sloping, and well laid-back, fine at points and clearly cut at the withers. Forelegs should be strong and straight-boned with joints in a correct alignment. Elbows hanging perpendicular to the body and working free of the sides.

BODY – The chest should be shallow, narrow and the front legs set not too widely apart, giving an athletic rather than a heavily chested appearance. As a guide only, the chest should be small enough to be easily spanned behind the shoulders by average hands, when the terrier is in a fit, working condition. The back should be strong, straight and, in comparison to the height of the terrier, give a balanced image. The loin should be slightly arched.

An exhibitor proudly shows off his brace of JRs.

HINDQUARTERS – Should be strong and muscular, well put together with good angulation and hand of stifle, giving plenty of drive and propulsion. Looking from behind, the hocks must be straight.

FEET – Round, hard padded, of cat-like appearance, neither turning in nor out.

TAIL – Should be set rather high, carried gaily and in proportion to the body length, usually about 10 cm (4 in) long, providing a good handhold.

COAT – Smooth, without being so sparse as not to provide a certain amount of protection from the elements and undergrowth. Rough or broken-coated without being woolly.

COLOUR – White should predominate with tan, black or brown markings. Brindle markings are unacceptable.

GAIT – Movement should be free, lively and well co-ordinated with straight action in front and behind.

NOTE
Dogs and bitches should be entire, and capable of breeding. Dogs should be shown to have two testicles fully descended into the scrotum.

A JR class in progress at Cruft's.

The standard for the Parson Jack Russell terrier

GENERAL APPEARANCE – Workmanlike, active and agile, built for speed and endurance.

CHARACTERISTICS – Essentially a working terrier with ability and conformation to go to ground and run with hounds.

TEMPERAMENT – Bold and friendly.

HEAD AND SKULL – Flat, moderately broad, gradually narrowing to the eyes. Shallow stop. Length from nose to stop slightly shorter than from stop to occiput. Nose black.

EYES – Almond-shaped, fairly deep-set, dark. Keen expression.

MOUTH – Jaws strong, muscular. Teeth with a perfect, regular and complete scissor bite, i.e. upper teeth closely overlapping the lower teeth and set square to the jaws.

NECK – Clean, muscular, of good length, gradually widening to the shoulders.

FOREQUARTERS – Shoulders strong and sloping, well laid-back, cleanly cut at withers. Legs strong, must be with joints turning neither in nor out. Elbows close to body, working free of sides.

BODY – Chest of moderate depth, capable of being spanned behind the shoulders by average-sized hands. Back strong and straight. Loin slightly arched. Well-balanced, length of back from withers to root of tail equal to height from withers to ground.

HINDQUARTERS – Strong, muscular, with good bend of stifle. Hocks short and parallel, giving plenty of drive.

FEET – Compact with firm pads, turning neither in nor out.

TAIL – Strong, straight, set on high. Customarily docked, with length complementing the body while providing a good handhold.

GAIT/MOVEMENT – Free, lively, well co-ordinated, straight action front and behind.

COAT – Naturally harsh, close and dense, whether rough or smooth. Belly and undersides coated. Skin must be thick and loose.

COLOUR – Entirely white, or predominantly white, with markings which are tan, lemon or black, or any combination of these colours, preferably confined to the head or root of tail.

SIZE – Height minimum 33 cm (13 in), ideally 35 cm (14 in) at withers for dogs, and minimum 30 cm (12 in), ideally 33 cm (13 in) at withers for bitches.

FAULTS – Any departure from the foregoing points should be regarded in exact proportion to its degree.

NOTE
Male animals should have two apparently normal testicles fully descended into the scrotum.

Parson Jack Russells awaiting judging at the world's largest dog show – Cruft's.

One wonders why it is the owner and not the JR who appears stressed while waiting for the class to be called to the ring at Cruft's.

Cruft's

Despite the fact that some JR owners and organisations are against Kennel Club registration of the breed, it would be remiss of me to not mention arguably the most famous dog show in the world – Cruft's, which is organised and run by the UK's Kennel Club.

The Kennel Club was founded in 1873 and, as mentioned in chapter 1 of this book, the Revd John Russell was a member from its inception until his death in 1883. The club came about due to Mr S.E. Shirley, the Member of Parliament for Ettington (Worcestershire), who called a meeting of the National Dog Club Committee. After lengthy discussions, 'twelve gentlemen' held the inaugural meeting of the Kennel Club at No. 2, Albert Mansions, Victoria Street, London on 4 April 1873.

From its inception, the club's idea was to become the ruling body of dog breeding in the UK. It organises shows, obedience tests, agility tests, field trials and working tests, registers dogs and their progeny, and sets the standards for all of the breeds which it recognises. The Kennel Club published its first Stud Book in 1873, and the book – edited by Frank Pearce, a journalist on *The Field* magazine, who wrote under the pen name of 'Idstone' – contained over 600 pages and the pedigrees of over 400 dogs.

At shows all around the UK, JR owners meet to both compete and exchange views.

105

The Kennel Club Committee put together a list of ten rules to govern dog shows, and only those breed clubs and societies which adopted and used these rules would be eligible for the Stud Book. The committee also ruled that all dogs shown at any 'unrecognised' shows would be disqualified from entry into the Stud Book, and denied entry at any Kennel Club shows.

In 1880, the Kennel Club introduced what they called 'a system of universal registration'; this system was very strongly opposed at first, but eventually accepted and remains with us today. In recent years, the Kennel Club has registered about 260,000 dogs each year. All Kennel Club registration is now computerised, and the Club's database currently contains over 4.7 million dog names, and is rising daily.

Charles Cruft was an entrepreneur who had a passion for dogs, and he began organising what he referred to as 'The Great Terrier Shows' in 1886, and he personally always regarded this as the first Cruft's dog show. The show was held at the Royal Aquarium, Windsor, England on 10–12 March 1886, and all the classes were for terriers. It is possible that some of the Parson's type of terriers may have taken part in this show.

The first Cruft's Dog Show for all breeds was held on 11–13 February 1891, at The Agricultural Hall, Islington, London, reputed to have been the best venue in London at that time. When he booked the Hall, Cruft did so for several years and insisted that no other dog shows be allowed to take place at that venue.

Today, Cruft's attracts almost 21,000 pedigree dogs each year, and costs the Kennel Club a staggering £2.3 million to set up and run. Almost 200 judges and almost 400 stewards help keep the show moving, and the show is now held at the UK's National Exhibition Centre (NEC) near Birmingham, England.

The points of the dog

1.	Nose	12.	Anus
2.	Muzzle	13.	Tail
3.	Foreface	14.	Thigh
4.	Eye	15.	Flank
5.	Stop	16.	Sheath
6.	Skull	17.	Hindleg
7.	Occiput	18.	Hock
8.	Ear	19.	Rear pastern
9.	Withers	20.	Paw
10.	Loins	21.	Stifle
11.	Rump or croup	22.	Abdomen

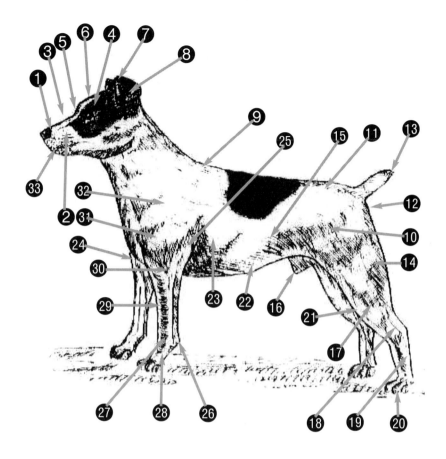

23.	Chest	29.	Forearm
24.	Brisket	30.	Forelimb
25.	Elbow	31.	Upper arm
26.	Stopper pad	32.	Shoulder
27.	Wrist	33.	Mouth
28.	Pastern		

The length of any dog is always measured from the point of his shoulder to the point of his buttock

The height of any dog is measured from the withers to the ground.

CHAPTER 7

DISEASES, AILMENTS AND FIRST AID

Properly cared for, the Jack Russell is an extremely healthy and hardy dog, and many owners never experience serious medical problems with any of their dogs. However, accidents can and do happen, and illness is certainly not unknown among JRs. Never take any risks, nor should you ignore anything 'out of the ordinary'; any unusual behaviour among your dogs should make you check more vigilantly, and you should always remember that no veterinary surgeon will mind being consulted for an animal which is not at death's door. It is better to act early, rather than wait until it is too late for anyone to be able to save your JR. Time waited is time wasted.

It is obviously impossible to list every disease and ailment that a JR could succumb to. I have, therefore, attempted to list the details of those diseases which are most likely to be encountered by the JR keeper, detailing the symptoms and probable treatment. Where possible, I have also indicated possible causes of the disease. None of this information should be seen as an alternative to treatment by a qualified vet, and in all cases of ill animals, particularly where that animal is very young or very old, you should not hesitate to contact your own veterinary surgeon.

Common diseases and ailments

Alopecia (hair loss)
This is often caused by the feeding of too many raw eggs, which contain a compound which inhibits biotin, resulting in this condition. There are also many other causes of hair loss in dogs, including seasonal environmental changes, and it is recommended that any JRs manifesting such symptoms be given a thorough examination by a qualified vet. See also 'Mites'.

Abscesses
Abscesses are simply wounds which have filled with pus, the bacteria *Staphylococcus* or *Streptococcus* being the usual cause. They can be caused by a variety of occurrences, such as bites or cuts. In order to prevent

wounds developing into abscesses, ensure that they are thoroughly cleaned and disinfected. Once abscesses have developed, they will need to be lanced and drained, often several times, and it may be necessary for the animal to be given a course of broad-spectrum antibiotics, such as ampicillin. Obviously, action of this type must only be taken by a qualified veterinary surgeon.

Bites and stings

These need to be split into four categories – insect, snake, rat and dog.

Insect bites (including stings)

Clip a little fur away from the area, so that you can actually see the problem, then wash with saline solution. Bees leave their sting in the victim, wasps do not. If there is a sting present, it should be carefully removed with tweezers and then the area wiped with cotton wool (or a cotton bud) soaked in alcohol, such as surgical spirit. For wasp stings, a little vinegar will prove beneficial, while for bee stings, use a little bicarbonate of soda. Dry the area thoroughly, and use an antihistamine spray or apply a wet compress to help reduce the irritation and swelling.

If your JR has been bitten or stung in the throat, veterinary attention must be sought as soon as possible; such stings can cause swelling that may block the airways and thus kill the dog.

Rat bites

Rat bites are one of the most dangerous of all bites that a JR may suffer; obviously working terriers are more likely to be bitten by a rat than others, but even the most pampered pet JR can find itself suffering this ignominy. Rats can carry many harmful diseases (including leptospirosis – which can be passed to humans – see 'Leptospirosis'), and so it is essential that no risks are taken.

Clip away the fur from around the wound, ensuring that the clippings do not become entangled in the wound itself. Wetting the scissors is recommended, as the hairs stick to the blades rather than falling onto the wound; dipping the scissors into a jug of water after each snip will remove all hairs from the metal. Thoroughly clean the area of the wound with a saline solution and then an antiseptic liquid; dry and apply liberal amounts of antiseptic wound-dusting powder. If the wound is large, or you have good reason to believe that the rat was infected, take the injured terrier to the vet as soon as possible after the injury, where the vet may well administer an injection of antibiotics. I would always recommend this action after any rat bite – better safe than sorry.

Snake bites

In the UK, there is only one species of venomous snake – the adder, or viper (*Viper berus*). Although it is unusual for dogs to be bitten by these reptiles, it does sometimes happen. During the spring or early summer, the snakes are rather lethargic, especially the gravid (pregnant) females. At such times, they will keep still as long as possible, even when approached. If your dog does not see the snake and stands on it, the snake will bite. This actually happened to one of my bitches, while we were walking in North Wales. At the time, neither I nor my wife noticed anything untoward; there had been a bit of a commotion in a bush, but we had assumed that the dogs had disturbed a rabbit. We were on our way back to the car at the time, and within five minutes, all three bitches with us were happily snuggled down in their cage in the back of our 4 × 4, and we headed for home. It took less than thirty minutes to get back home and, when I opened the cage door, I knew something was seriously amiss. While the other two bitches leapt out as normal, Belle, the oldest, did not move, but merely looked at me. I tried to persuade her to jump out, but to no avail, and so I lifted her out. Immediately I lifted her, I saw her front left paw – it was twice the normal size. I quickly carried her into the house, where my wife took down our canine first-aid kit, and began snipping fur off the afflicted paw. It was not long before we found four teeth marks; we knew that she had been bitten by a snake. We rang our veterinary surgeon, who told us to keep the bitch calm, and get her round to the surgery as soon as possible.

When we arrived, Belle was obviously feeling very sorry for herself, and the vet confirmed that she had been bitten by an adder. The next 48 hours were the longest I ever remember. To cut the story short, Belle survived the bite, and went on to live a long and active life.

If one of your JRs gets bitten by an adder, it is most important that you keep the injured animal as calm as possible (and you must also remain calm, as your actions will influence the animal), and seek immediate medical attention.

Dog bites

It is a fact that many JRs will suffer from bites from other dogs, be they JRs or some other breed. The treatment for dog bites should be the same as that for any other type of bite, with care taken to prevent the wound from becoming infected; if necessary, consult your veterinary surgeon. Also, remember that, if two or more dogs are fighting, it is unwise to simply step in and expect the dogs to desist. It is very likely that, if you follow this course of action, you – and any other human trying the same tactics – will be injured by the dogs.

Once you have managed to stop the fight, and the dogs have calmed down enough to allow you to examine their wounds, you should engage the assistance of another person to hold the dog while you examine it. When the wounds are found, the area of the bite must be clipped of fur, and the wound thoroughly washed with a saline solution followed by an antiseptic liquid. A good dusting with an antiseptic wound powder will finish the job. If action is not taken, the wound may fester and result in abscesses.

Bleeding

Most lay people are not used to seeing blood, and a little blood often appears to be 'gallons'; this often frightens the dog's owner, and in their panic, mistakes can easily be made. *Never* apply tourniquets to any limb. See *'Cuts'*.

Botulism

Botulism is a killer. The disease is caused by one of the most common bacteria known to science, *Clostridium botulinum*, usually 'Type C', a natural contaminant of most wild bird cadavers. When this bacterium comes into contact with any decaying flesh (i.e. meat), it causes a deadly toxin to be formed. If this flesh is then eaten by an animal, the toxin affects its victim by attacking the animal's nervous system, causing paralysis, at first usually in the hind legs. Eventually, this paralysis will affect the body's vital organs, and leads inevitably to the death of the affected animal. There is no cure or treatment for this, and dogs are among the most susceptible animals to botulism.

In order to try to prevent this deadly disease, pay particular attention to the meat that you feed; defrost frozen meat and feed immediately. If there is any doubt whatsoever about the meat, boil it for at least fifteen minutes before feeding. Botulism is not contagious and sometimes only one animal of a group may succumb to the illness. If for whatever reason you believe that your dogs have a high risk of this disease, it is possible to have an annual toxoid injection to provide some protection for them.

Breathing problems

Dogs gasping for breath are obviously showing symptoms of some form of breathing difficulty; this may be heat-stroke (see 'Heat-Stroke'), fluid on the lungs, infectious respiratory disease (see later) or an obstruction of some kind. Obstructions can be removed from a dog's mouth with a finger.

Artificial respiration, though difficult, is possible with dogs. If a JR has stopped breathing, rather than give mouth-to-mouth respiration, hold the animal by its hind legs and, keeping your arms straight, swing the animal to left and then to right. This transfers the weight of the dog's internal organs onto and off the diaphragm, causing the lungs to fill with and empty of air. Keep this up until the dog begins breathing on its own, help arrives, or you believe the dog to be beyond help.

111

Contagious respiratory disease ('kennel cough')

This disease is usually caused by an infection involving several viruses and a bacteria (*Bordetella bronchiseptica*), and is spread by direct contact with infected dogs. This is most common in kennels, where many dogs are in contact with each other, hence its common name.

Symptoms include a persistent, dry hacking cough, and the severity of the disease depends on the viruses involved. Although not life-threatening, even with the correct treatment – cough suppressants and antibiotics – full recovery may take several weeks.

Convulsions

Convulsions are a symptom, an indication that the dog has an infection of some kind or has been poisoned, and NOT a disease. There are obviously many possible causes of convulsions, and one of the most common is heat-stroke. However, if your JR is suffering from convulsions, you should contact your veterinary surgeon, and seek urgent medical attention for the ailing animal.

Cuts, abrasions and other wounds

There are several different types of wound which a dog may suffer, and each requires a slightly different technique.

INCISED (CLEAN) CUTS

These are straight cuts, as one would get from a sharp knife blade; as such, they bleed profusely. This bleeding, which can be very frightening to people not used to such things – a little blood appears as 'gallons' to most lay people, even though there may only be a thimble full – helps clean the wound of debris, and this lessens the possibility of infection.

Bleeding should be stemmed by direct pressure, if at all possible; where it is not, apply indirect pressure on an artery at the heart side of the wound. Elevating the injury will enable gravity to help reduce the blood flow. Apply a suitable dressing; large and/or deep cuts will almost certainly require sutures (stitches) from a qualified vet. If the cut will not cease bleeding, consult your veterinary surgeon.

LACERATED CUTS

These are tears in the skin, as caused by barbed wire, for instance, and will bleed less profusely than incised cuts. The big danger is that the injury will have pushed dirt and debris into the wound, and the lack of bleeding will mean that the dirt is not washed out. You must clean the wound with a saline solution (salt water – one teaspoonful of table salt to one litre of warm water); dry it and apply dressing if necessary.

CONTUSIONS (BRUISES)
These are signs of internal bleeding, and a careful watch must be kept on the injured animal. If shock sets in, seek veterinary advice immediately.

PUNCTURES (STAB WOUNDS)
Puncture wounds, which can be caused by nails, slivers of wood and other such objects, usually appear very small on the surface but, of course, could be very deep. NEVER remove any object from a wound, as this may aggravate the injury and/or allow large amounts of bleeding. Apply pressure around the wound site, using a dressing to maintain the pressure, and seek medical attention from a qualified veterinary surgeon immediately.

GUNSHOT WOUNDS
If you work your JR, it is possible that he may be accidentally shot. The most common type of wound to a working terrier is likely to be from a shotgun, in which case the animal will be peppered with balls of shot, which

A young owner/handler tries to keep both himself and his JR amused while awaiting their turn in the ring.

will all require removal; bleeding should not be profuse. The other type of wound is from a solid projectile, i.e. a bullet. Bullets make two wounds – one on entry and one on exit. Where sporting (hollow point) ammunition is used, the exit wound will be several times larger than the entry wound.

In all cases of gunshot wound, stem the flow of blood, keep the animal calm, checking for signs of trauma, and seek veterinary treatment immediately.

Dental problems

Dogs, like humans, have teeth, and also, like humans, occasionally have dental problems. They may sometimes damage their teeth; gingivitis, a gum disorder, is also quite common in all breeds of dog. The build-up of food debris on the teeth often leads to dental problems, and the diet of the JR is, therefore, an important factor in the condition of the teeth. Any problems with a terrier's teeth must be treated by a properly qualified vet.

Regular cleaning of the JR's teeth with a canine toothpaste will help reduce the risk of dental problems, and also reduce the incidence of halitosis (bad breath). Feeding your JR regularly with hard, crunchy food, biscuits or bones, will also help clean the teeth.

Diarrhoea

Diarrhoea is a symptom and NOT a disease; it is indicative of a problem, which may be serious or minor, but will still require investigation. In JRs, this condition is often referred to as the 'scours', and is usually, but of course not always, a sign that the animal has been fed on a poor diet, or its food is contaminated. A sudden and abrupt change of diet will almost always cause diarrhoea, as will the feeding of food which has 'gone off'. Diarrhoea can also be indicative of some other, more serious affliction, such as poisoning, internal parasites or even stress.

If you are feeding your JRs a proper, balanced diet of good quality food, they should not suffer from loose motions as a matter of course. One must remember, however, that some dogs gain allergies to certain food or food additives, and this should always be borne in mind. Once you have found a good diet which suits your JRs, stick to it.

Diarrhoea must never be ignored, or considered as 'normal'. It causes the animal to dehydrate, and can lead to irreparable body damage (particularly of the kidneys), and even death. You should isolate the affected JR and keep it on a water and electrolyte regime for 24 hours, dosing with kaolin solution about every two hours. After the fast, food intake should be gradually built up again; do NOT put the animal straight back on its original diet, otherwise the whole problem may recur. Chicken, rabbit and fish are excellent 'invalid' foods, and ideal for this task.

It is possible to purchase salts to make up a re-hydrating fluid, but where

Dogs' teeth should be inspected regularly . . .

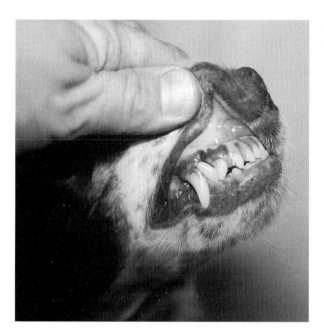

. . . and, if necessary, cleaned.

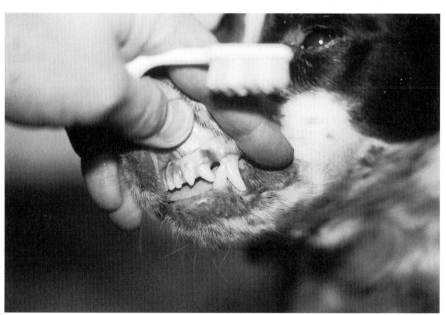

this is not available, it is easy to make one from normal household ingredients; simply add one teaspoonful of salt and one tablespoonful of sugar to one litre of warm water.

If the diarrhoea persists, or if there is blood in the motions, the vet must be consulted immediately.

Distemper, Canine (CD) ('hard pad')

Canine distemper is caused by a virus, and is one of the most common fatal diseases in dogs. Other dogs are the most common source of such an infection, with the incubation period being between 7 and 9 days. In some countries, including the UK, owners routinely have their animals vaccinated against this disease as a matter of course, while in others this does not happen. I cannot recommend too strongly that all dogs should receive their vaccination against canine distemper, and this should be 'topped up' every twelve months.

Symptoms of the disease are swollen feet, leading to hard pad, the actual

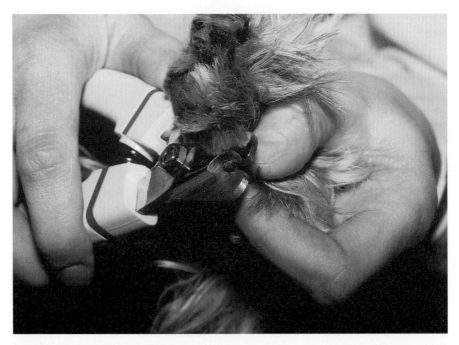

If a dog's claws grow over-long, they will need to be clipped. It is vital that guidance is sought by the novice before such tasks are undertaken, since cutting the claws incorrectly can cause distress to the dog concerned.

thickening of the soles of the feet and a classic sign of distemper infection, runny eyes and nose, diarrhoea, lack of appetite, a larger than average thirst and a rash, usually under the chin. In its latter stages, the infected animal will vomit, have convulsions and, shortly before dying, will pass into a coma.

This disease is highly contagious and, at the first signs of distemper, all infected dogs must be isolated. Ensure that you thoroughly disinfect your hands after handling a sick animal; it is all too easy to spread infection. Immediate veterinary advice must be sought, although only very mild cases can be treated; it is often kinder, both to the infected dog and the others in your care, to have the affected animal put down once the diagnosis is confirmed by a vet.

Enteritis

Enteritis is an inflammation of the intestines, causing diarrhoea, and is very common among puppies and young dogs. If your JR is experiencing diarrhoea, and shows signs of blood in his motions, this may indicate this condition. It can be caused by different things but, usually, it is the bacterium *Escherichia coli*, often referred to by its abbreviated name of *E.coli*, and formerly known to science as *Bacillus coli*. Immediate treatment with a broad-spectrum antibiotic, supplemented with regular doses of kaolin, may cure this condition. If left untreated, the affected animal will most definitely die.

Another major cause of enteritis is *Campylobacter*; in humans, this type of 'food poisoning' is known as dysentery. The most effective antibiotics for use against this are chloramphenicol and gentamicin.

As mentioned under the heading of 'Diarrhoea', affected animals must be given large amounts of water and electrolyte to avoid the dangers of dehydration.

Fractures

Fractures are caused by either direct or indirect pressure on the bones, which may crack or actually break. Where the bone is broken and pierces the skin, this is known as an open or compound fracture, and all others as closed fractures. Signs of such injury are obvious – painful movement of the limb, tenderness, swelling, loss of control of the limb, deformity of the limb, unnatural movement of the limb, and crepitus (the sensation or, in very bad cases, the sound of the two ends of the bones grinding on each other).

Keep the patient quiet, and steady and support the injured limb, immobilising it with bandages and splints if necessary, to prevent it moving and causing greater damage. Raising the limb will help reduce discomfort and swelling (by reducing the blood flow).

Veterinary treatment must be sought for all cases of (suspected) fractures.

'Hard pad'
see 'Canine Distemper'

Heat-stroke

Dogs cannot tolerate high temperatures, reacting adversely to too much heat, and may well die from heat-stroke, often referred to by 'old timers' as 'the sweats', a rather misleading term, since dogs cannot sweat. As in all things, prevention is better than cure, and the siting of the kennel (as discussed in an earlier chapter) is very important. In the confines of a motor car, the temperature can quickly rise to a dangerous level, even in the cooler sunshine of autumn and spring. No animals should be left unattended in a vehicle, or transported in such a manner that they are in full sunlight. It must be remembered that the sun does not stay in the same position throughout the day, and that, even if the car is in the shadows when you leave it, it may not stay that way for long. When you return, your precious JRs may well be dead.

In extreme summer temperatures, or in areas where it is known that temperature will be high, every effort must be made to insulate the JR's kennel, and ensure that it is built in an area where it and its inmates are protected from the full effect of varying temperatures. Where it is not possible to keep the kennel as cool as one would like, wet cloths may be hung over the kennel itself to keep the temperature down, although they will soon dry out, and so require constant attention throughout the day. Placing bricks on each corner of the kennel roof, and then positioning a piece of timber over them, will act as 'double glazing', and will be extremely effective in reducing heat build-up in the kennel. However, if due consideration is given to this aspect of husbandry and management at the design and build stages, the problem should not occur.

The first sign of heat-stroke or heat exhaustion is an agitated JR in obvious distress. If in their kennel, affected dogs will stretch out and pant heavily; if left untreated, they will eventually collapse, pass into a coma and die.

Immediately a dog shows symptoms of heat-stroke, you must act – quickly; delay can be fatal. The dog's body is overheating, and so your first task must be to lower its body temperature. With mildly affected dogs, simply moving them to a cool area, and ensuring a steady passage of cool air over them, is usually effective; a light spraying with cold water from a plant mister is also beneficial. In bad cases, where it is literally make or break, I find that the best method is to immerse the animal to the neck in a bath of cold water, repeating this procedure regularly for the next few minutes, by which time the dog should be showing signs of recovery. If a hose pipe is available, use this to cover the afflicted dog with a fine mist of cold water; never direct a high-powered stream of water at any dog.

Ensure that the terrier is thoroughly dried, and placed in a cool area, with a small amount of bedding; this bedding will also help to dry the dog's coat.

This is a very drastic 'treatment', and should only be attempted where the animal is very badly affected.

In all cases, it is vital to keep the head cool, because brain death can occur, as the brain is quite literally 'cooked'. The best analogy for this is to imagine the JR's brain as a raw egg, and then imagine what happens to a raw egg when it is subjected to heat – it solidifies.

Veterinary advice should be sought at the earliest opportunity for all affected dogs.

Hypocalcaemia ('milk fever')

A lack of calcium in the blood, this affliction can occur in any nursing bitch, but is more likely in those bitches with large litters. This affliction is characterised by convulsions; muscle tremors and ataxia (an irregular gait or staggering, caused by incoordination of the muscles) are common symptoms. The cause of hypocalcaemia in such cases is usually a poor diet. Always ensure that you feed a complete, balanced diet and, where pregnant or nursing bitches are concerned, ensure that the phosphorous–calcium ratio is correct (see chapter 4 'Feeding'). In all cases, you should consult your veterinary surgeon immediately; he will probably administer an intraperitoneal injection of calcium borogluconate, which gives a speedy

In the ring at Cruft's, a JR awaits the judge's scrutiny.

119

response in affected animals. After this injection, a calcium-rich diet is essential for total recovery.

Infectious canine hepatitis

The symptoms of infectious canine hepatitis may include bloody diarrhoea, anorexia, depression and abdominal pains. The disease is caused by a virus, and your JR may become infected through direct or indirect (e.g. via saliva, urine, faeces of the other dog) contact with an infected dog. As the virus can survive outside a dog's body for up to ten days, it is very easy for your dog to come into contact with infected parts of the environment. As there is no specific treatment for this disease, it is highly recommended that all dogs are vaccinated against the risk.

Kennel cough
See 'Contagious respiratory disease'

Leptospirosis, canine

Often called 'rat-catcher's yellows' or 'Weil's disease', leptospirosis is zoonotic, and so can be transmitted to humans, and the disease is often fatal. It is caused by two bacteria, and the life cycle of these bacteria may well cause severe damage to an infected JR's kidneys and liver.

Wild rats can, and usually do, carry many diseases. One of the most common is Weil's disease, or leptospirosis (sometimes called leptospiral jaundice), or commonly known as 'rat-catcher's yellows'. This is caused by spirochaetes, a type of bacteria. In common with other bacteria, once this enters an animal's bloodstream (perhaps through a cut or graze on the hand), it causes a fever, produces toxic substances and can sometimes kill. For some reason, as yet unknown, these bacteria do not affect the host animal, the rat, which is therefore known as a passive carrier. It is thought that the rat and the spirochaetes may have evolved together, since the bacteria require a host animal in which they can survive and which they do not damage, in order that the bacteria themselves are not wiped out. Some of the bacteria are passed out in the rat's urine and all that is needed is for an animal (or human) to get some of that urine on a cut or graze, and he is infected. Likewise, eating food with hands soiled with rat urine (for example, after a successful foray against *Rattus norwegicus*) is a sure way of infecting one's body with these bacteria.

The first symptoms of leptospirosis appear within a few days of the infection. Fevers, diarrhoea, severe thigh pains and vomiting are some of these symptoms. Within a week, the victim is jaundiced, owing to liver damage. It is usually at this stage that the family doctor is given some indication of the nature of the illness and, if he is to treat the patient successfully, he must move quickly, since if he does not, and the patient's own immune system is not strong, the patient may be dead within the next seven to ten days. This information is not intended to frighten the reader, merely to warn of the possible dangers of hunting the rat. These dangers can be minimised by always wearing strong rubber gloves at all times when hunting rats, and also by adhering to a strict hygiene routine, i.e. always washing hands well before eating or drinking.

Some years ago, I was awakened in the middle of the night by searing pains and chronic diarrhoea and when, a few days later I looked at my reflection in the mirror, I saw a bright yellow face staring back at me, I realised that I was jaundiced, and made arrangements to see my local doctor. He took blood samples and sent them off for analysis, ordering me to rest until I returned for the results a few days later. The results were positive and the doctor informed me that I had a mild case of hepatitis. There was no real treatment, he told me, only rest.

I returned home and tried to do just that. It was during this time that, being totally bored, I sent a friend to the library to fetch some books which might help while away the time. Knowing my interest in country sports and particularly in terriers, my friend brought a selection of appropriate books back for me. One of them was by Brian Plummer and gave instructions on working terriers, along with more than a few interesting little stories. The bit

Let us out – we've got work to do!

that I found interesting, however, almost scared me to death. In graphic detail, Mr Plummer described an illness where all of the symptoms matched mine. He did not, however, refer to the disease as hepatitis, but as leptospirosis – Weil's disease. I have never had my own diagnosis confirmed, my doctor merely said that it was a possibility but, as I had been hunting rats a few days before the onset of my illness, I have no doubt that I had had a mild attack of Weil's disease. It took many months before I was fighting fit again and, so concerned did I become by the thought that the disease could have killed me, that I have never hunted rats since.

If, despite this dire warning, you are still intent on hunting the rat with your JRs, there are precautions that you should take if you are to avoid the risk of contracting one of the many diseases that wild rats can, and very often do, carry. As stated earlier, strong, well fitting rubber gloves should be worn at all times. The heavy duty rubber gloves sold in hardware stores are ideal. If they are too bulky, or do not fit well, they will quickly become a nuisance and, shortly after that has happened, you will stop wearing them.

Your JR must also be protected, although protective garments for him are just not on. It is, however, possible (and advisable) to have all of your animals vaccinated against leptospirosis and other rat-borne diseases. After all, prevention is better than cure. Even so, it is still often necessary to carry out first aid treatment on your JR if you do use him for hunting, or even if he just decides to hunt rats himself.

After every hunting trip, dogs must be closely examined (while you are still wearing your rubber gloves) for any cuts or abrasions; these must be thoroughly cleaned with a good antiseptic. To do this, it will be necessary for some of the JR's fur to be clipped off. After washing well, dry by dabbing with a piece of cotton wool and then apply some wound dusting powder (available from your local veterinary surgeon). It is always best to take any seriously injured animal to the vet at the earliest possible opportunity. The vet will decide if any antibiotics are required.

Your JR should be given a good bath a short time after any contact with wild rats. Not only will this help to reduce the risk of infection from any rat urine which has been put on the coat of the animal, it will also help you to notice any cuts or abrasions which may otherwise have gone unnoticed.

In young puppies, leptospirosis may manifest itself in the sudden death of one or more of the pups in the litter, often without any prior indication of ill health. Symptoms vary, but may include anorexia, lethargy, jaundice, vomiting, diarrhoea or haemorrhaging. In acute cases, even where the correct treatment has been given, death may result within a few hours of the onset of symptoms. Always seek veterinary advice in any cases where this disease may be involved, and ensure that your dogs are properly vaccinated against the risks, keeping those vaccinations up to date with yearly booster shots.

Mange
See 'Mites'

Mastitis
This is the inflammation of the bitch's mammary glands, and often occurs when she is in the early stages of feeding young. It is a very painful condition that requires immediate medical attention. The glands become very swollen and hard and the puppies can obtain very little – if any – milk. Unless it is cleared up quickly, the pups will probably die (unless you step in and hand rear them) and the bitch will, at best, be very ill. The disease is caused by infection by *E. coli* and treatment usually consists of antibiotics, preferably ampicillin.

Mites
Mites have unpleasant effects on dogs, and there are three types commonly found on the animal:

Sarcoptes scabiei causes two types of mange in dogs, which can become infected through direct contact with other infected animals, such as rodents, or simply by being on infected ground. One type of mange causes alopecia and pruritus (an intense itching), while the other causes only foot or toe problems ('foot rot').

The first sign of mange is persistent scratching, even though there is no obvious cause such as fleas. Eventually, the skin will become very red and sore, a symptom that is easier to notice in the white areas of the JR's coat. As the disease progresses, these sores cause baldness and the sores become even worse.

A parasiticidal wash (e.g. bromocyclen) must be applied to the affected areas, or injections of ivermectin administered; this drug cannot be used in the first month of pregnancy, or it will cause congenital defects. The living quarters must be thoroughly treated, soaking everything in a strong solution of disinfectant or bleach, which must be washed off before any dog is returned to the kennel.

Be warned – mange can be contracted by humans, when it is known as scabies.

Otodectes cynotis, ear mites, are common in dogs and can easily be treated with ear drops which contain gamma BHC, or with ivermectin injections. If your JR seems to spend a lot of time scratching his ears, an investigation is called for; if you are not experienced at looking for such afflictions, get a more experienced JR breeder to help, or take the dog to your local veterinary surgeon.

A build-up of wax in the ears, dotted with black specks, is a sure indication that a JR has ear mites; the black specks are probably spots of dried blood. The ear mites are usually white or colourless and are not visible to the naked eye – a magnifying lens or otoscope being required. If left untreated, the irritation caused by these mites will cause the dog to scratch, sometimes until its ears actually bleed. The mites can move down the aural canal and infect the middle ear; such an infection will cause the affected animal to lose its sense of balance. This may be indicated either by the terrier simply being unable to hold his head straight or, in more serious cases, by constantly falling over.

It is important that all animals that have been in contact with the infected terrier are also treated, as ear mites can infect other animals who may not show any symptoms for some time.

Seek veterinary advice in all cases of ear mite, loss of balance etc.

Trombicula autumnalis, the harvest mite, can cause sores on the underside of the neck and trunk of dogs, particularly during the autumn period; a wash in a bromocyclen-based product will be effective.

Parasites

Even the most pampered JR can suffer from the unwanted attentions of parasites, either internal (endoparasites) or external (ectoparasites). JRs can suffer from both tape worms (*cestodes*) and round worms (*nematodes*). The species which may infect your JR are *Echinococcus granulosus, Dipylidium caninum* and various species of the genus *Taenia*. Although the sight of the tapeworm segments which an infected dog will show in its faeces may be repugnant to the dog's owner, the presence of these endoparasites is not usually a problem to the host animal (your JR). The presence of such beasties does, however, indicate a problem with infection, as the tapeworm cysts can cause disease.

The most common tapeworm afflicting both dogs and cats in the UK is *Dipylidium caninum*, and the intermediate host of this helminth is the flea or the louse. The presence of small rice grain-like segments around the anus of the dog, or in its faeces, is a sure indication of *Dipylidium caninum* infestation. Control of this parasite involves treating the existing infection plus eliminating flea and/or louse problems in the animals concerned. This is the only effective method of breaking the transmission cycle.

The nematodes are round worms, most of which have a direct life cycle, i.e. they do not need an intermediate host, unlike the tapeworms. This group of endoparasites includes *Toxocara canis*, a parasite which is linked with health problems in humans, particularly in children.

Heart worms (*Dirofilaria immitis*), hookworms (*Uncinaria stenocephala*), whipworms (*Trichuris vulpis*), bladder and liver worms (*Capillaria* spp.) and *lungworms (Aelurostrongylus abstrusus, Angiostrongylus vasorum)*, and *Oslerus osleri* (formerly known to science as *Filaroides osleri*) are also some-

Life cycle of the flea

Adult flea on the JR (circa 3 mm long).

⇊

Eggs are laid about two days after the female flea's first feed on the animal.

⇊

Eggs drop off the JR's coat and into the environment.

⇊

Between two and fourteen days after being laid, eggs hatch,
and larvae are produced.

⇊

Larvae have two moults.

⇊

Larvae pupate (this takes about seven days in optimum conditions).

⇊

The cocoon is covered in environmental debris.

⇊

Adult flea emerges after ten days. More may emerge for several
months after pupation.

⇊

Cycle repeats *ad infinitum.*

times found. Veterinary examination, and clinical investigation of the faeces will be necessary to positively identify the actual problem.

Although not always manifesting itself as a physical problem, the first signs of a worm infestation are usually an insatiable appetite coupled with a steady loss of weight. Sometimes, segments of the worms may be found in the terrier's faeces before other symptoms indicate a problem. Seek veterinary advice. A vet will prescribe an anthelmintic (an agent which is destructive to worms i.e. a wormer) such as mebendazole or fenbenzadole.

Fleas are a common ectoparasite; they bite their host and then feed on the blood which appears at the bite site. This area will show an inflammatory reaction, and will obviously cause a certain amount of irritation to the terrier. In some terriers, these areas will show severe lesions, and this indicates that the animal has become sensitised to allergens in the flea saliva. This affliction is referred to as 'flea allergic dermatitis' in dogs.

Identification of the flea can be carried out by the appearance of the flea's head, where the presence or otherwise of 'combs' is used to identify the species. By far the most common flea to infect dogs is the so-called 'cat flea', *Ctenocephalides felis*, although they may be infected with the dog flea (*Ctenocephalides canis*), particularly so in situations where there is no presence of, nor contact with, cats.

Ticks

By far the most common types of tick to affect dogs in the UK are the sheep tick (*Ixodes ricinus*), and the hedgehog tick (*Ixodes hexagonus*). Ticks are external parasites that most JRs will catch at some stage, especially if used for hunting. These ectoparasites may be contracted from other dogs, or from other animal species including cats, rabbits and other such species. Insecticidal preparations are readily available from veterinary surgeons, and should be applied, as per the vet's instructions, as soon as possible after the infestation has been identified.

When an infestation of ticks has been discovered on your JR, all of his bedding must be removed and, preferably, burned, and the kennel thoroughly disinfected. Use 'tick powder' as a prophylactic (preventative measure) to treat all bedding and even the kennel itself. Do *not* use such powders and sprays in cases where a bitch is still feeding her puppies, unless the veterinary surgeon gives absolute assurances that it is suitable for this kind of use. With most of these powders, there is a danger of poisoning the litter.

Ticks are rather more difficult to deal with than fleas, but they do respond to some sprays and powders, although in some countries these may only be available from veterinary surgeons. Care must be taken to ensure that the mouth parts of ticks are completely removed from the dog's skin, otherwise infection and abscesses can occur; never simply pull ticks out. Paint alcohol on the tick using a fine paint brush, and the tick should have died and dropped off within 24 hours; if not, simply repeat the process.

Although some authorities suggest that ticks be burned off with a lighted cigarette, this should never be attempted. It is all too easy to burn the dog with the cigarette and the alcohol method is much more effective, with none of the dangers.

There are now a number of devices on the market which have been specifically designed to remove ticks, mainly because of concern regarding Lyme's disease in humans. Among these is a type of sprung forceps which grip the tick around the head; the device is then gently twisted backwards and forwards, until the tick comes out. I have tested several such implements, and have had 100% success with each; I now always keep one in my kennel first-aid kit.

Parvovirus, canine

Severe bloody diarrhoea and vomiting are symptoms which may indicate that your JR has contracted canine parvovirus. In young puppies, in particular, this diarrhoea is extremely dangerous, leading to acute dehydration very quickly. It important that all puppies showing such symptoms are taken to a qualified veterinary surgeon as soon as possible. Although there is no specific treatment for this disease, your vet will be able to treat the puppy for secondary infections, such as the diarrhoea, caused by the disease.

The disease itself is caused by a virus, which can be transmitted either directly or indirectly to your JR from an infected dog. The virus can, in ideal circumstances, survive in the environment for up to six months.

Ensuring that your JR is vaccinated and given regular boosters will help him avoid this disease.

Pyometra

This is the accumulation of pus within the uterus; when it occurs, it is mainly (but not solely) in older bitches, and often after the start of a pseudo-pregnancy. Organisms responsible for this condition in dogs include *Streptococcus, Staphylococcus, E. coli, Corynebacterium*.

Affected bitches will be anorexic, lethargic, and will often have a fever. Medical attention must be sought immediately, as the uterus may rupture, causing peritonitis, and an ovariohysterectomy will be required urgently.

Rabies

In countries where this disease is prevalent, dogs can become infected and, arguably, are the main carriers of the disease. Clinical signs of the disease include lethargy, posterior paralysis and anxiety; recovery of infected dogs is not usual.

With the UK's quarantine laws about to change at the time of writing, and become far more relaxed, I fear that we may again see cases of this awful disease on our shores. It is in no-one's interest to import dogs which may be carrying this disease. It is to be hoped that the new 'pet passport' system will prove more effective than many pet owners, kennel proprietors and veterinary surgeons fear. (See the chapter on 'The New Quarantine Laws for the UK'.)

Ringworm (Dermatophytosis)

This is a fungal infection of the material which forms hair, nails and skin – keratin. It may be contracted by contact with an infected dog or cat; long-haired cats, in particular, while appearing normal, may well carry this infection. Caused by the fungus *Microsporum canis*, or *Trichophyton menta-grophytes*, this disease is not caused by a worm, as many are led to believe by its name. The condition manifests itself with hair loss and bald, scaly patches

of skin. Home treatment is sometimes successful, but it is strongly recommended that veterinary advice is sought. As the condition is transmissible to man, it must be treated immediately.
See also 'Mites'.

Sarcoptic mange
See 'Mites'

Scours
See 'Diarrhoea'

Shock

Shock, which is an acute fall in blood pressure, is often evident after the terrier has been involved in an accident or has been injured; certain diseases can also cause this condition. It manifests itself with cool skin, pale lips and gums (due to the lack of circulation); faint, rapid pulse; staring but unseeing eyes.

The victim must be kept warm and the blood circulation returned to normal as soon as possible. Massaging the JR will help circulation, and wrapping it in a towel or blanket will help keep it warm. The affected animal should be kept quiet and warm, and veterinary treatment sought as soon as possible.

Urolithiasis (gall stones)

Varying in size from a particle of sand to quite a large stone, gall stones sometimes occur in Jack Russells. Treatment consists of antibiotics, surgery and the use of special diets to dissolve the stone. Veterinary treatment is essential.

In many cases, health problems are avoidable, and the best way to ensure healthy terriers is to indulge in good husbandry, including the provision of an adequate, balanced diet. If you suspect your JR is 'sickening', contact your veterinary surgeon without delay; time waited is time wasted.

The basics of first aid

The old saying that things are as easy as ABC is very true when it comes to first aid, the ABC being – AIRWAYS, BREATHING, CIRCULATION. In other words, if the patient is not breathing, get the airways clear before you try to get the animal breathing, and only once the animal is breathing should you concern yourself with the other symptoms, e.g. bleeding, fractures and burns.

All first aid principles are the same, regardless of species involved, and I cannot recommend too highly that everyone should have a basic training in the subject. In the UK, such organisations as the Red Cross and the St John's

Ambulance Service run courses at very reasonable rates, and going on one may help you save a life, human or canine.

I have found two widely used definitions for first aid, which I feel help to explain the subject:

'First aid is the skilled application of accepted principles of treatment, on the occurrence of an accident, or in the case of a sudden illness, using facilities and materials available at the time.'

'First aid is the approved method of treating a casualty until they are placed, if necessary, in the care of a qualified medical practitioner, or removed to a hospital.'

The objects of first aid are threefold – to sustain life, to prevent the patient's condition worsening, and to promote the patient's recovery. The methods used are:

a. Assess the situation
b. Diagnose the condition
c. Treat immediately and adequately

Remember to ensure your own safety at all times.

Prevention is, of course, better than cure. Ensure that your JR is given a good, balanced diet, his kennel cleaned regularly, he is not subjected to extremes of temperatures, is kept away from draughts, and is not stressed unnecessarily. Any cuts, abrasions or bites must be cleaned and treated immediately.

First aid

Some of the most common dog injuries – minor cuts and abrasions – occur when the animal is going about its daily routine, or is being worked, and it is important that they are treated as soon as possible, in order to minimise adverse effects on the animal. In order to do this, a small first-aid kit should be kept in or near the kennel, and taken along on every outing. You should, of course, also have the necessary skills and experience to treat these minor injuries. If there is any doubt as to the seriousness of the injuries, or the dog's general condition, veterinary treatment should be sought as soon as practical.

A suitable first-aid kit for terriers should contain the following items as a minimum, and should always accompany you on any trip, and be near at hand at all times. Personal taste, skills and preferences, tempered by experience will dictate the actual contents of your kit, but ensure that once an item has been used, it is replaced *before* it is needed again.

1. NAIL CLIPPERS
   These should be top quality, and can be used for trimming the dog's nails. Use the type which work on the guillotine principle, where one blade hits the other, rather than on the scissors principle, which can result in nails being pulled out.

2. TWEEZERS
   For the removal of foreign bodies. Ensure that these have rounded ends, in order to minimise the risk of injury to the dog.

3. SCISSORS
   These should be curved and round-ended, and are to be used to cut off the fur around any wound. They must *not* be used for trimming nails.

4. ANTISEPTIC LOTION
   For cleansing cuts, wounds and abrasions.

5. ANTIHISTAMINE
   Occasionally, a terrier will be stung by a bee, wasp or other such insect. The sting should be removed and antihistamine applied. (see 'Bites and stings'.)

6. COTTON WOOL
   Used for cleaning wounds, cuts and abrasions, and for stemming the flow of blood.

7. SURGICAL GAUZE
   Used for padding wounds and stemming the flow of blood.

8. ADHESIVE PLASTERS
   Although these will soon be chewed off by the dog, they are useful for applying directly to small wounds and for keeping dressings in place. They can also be used for minor splinting.

9. BANDAGES
   A selection of small bandages should be kept for binding broken limbs and wounds. They will, of course, be temporary, as the dog will chew them off.

10. COTTON BUDS
    Ideal for cleaning wounds and the application of ointments etc. With care, they can also be used to clean the pinnae (ear flaps) but UNDER NO CIRCUMSTANCES should you poke these (or any other object) down the ear canal.

11. TABLE SALT
    A solution of table salt (one teaspoonful of salt to one litre of water) is a good solution to wash debris from wounds and counter infection. One teaspoon of salt mixed in one litre of warm water with one tablespoonful of sugar or glucose makes an excellent re-hydrating fluid for terriers.

12. SODIUM BICARBONATE
    On a wet compress, this will help reduce swelling.

13. ALCOHOL (SURGICAL SPIRIT)
    Useful for the removal of ticks etc.

14. STYPTIC PENCIL
    To help stem the flow of blood.

15. ELIZABETHAN COLLAR
    Useful (to try) to prevent a terrier from interfering with dressings, sutures etc.

Many of the items listed can be used on either canine *or* human injuries.

If in any doubt about the physical treatment of your JR, consult a qualified veterinary surgeon who will be happy to advise you on the best course of action for both yourself and your terrier.

Zoonotic diseases

A zoonosis (plural zoonoses) is a disease which can be transmitted from animal species to humans, often with dire and sometimes fatal results. There are many such diseases, and I list below some of them:

- Fleas
- Ringworm
- Sarcoptic mange
- Salmonellosis
- Leptospirosis
- Toxoplasmosis
- *Toxocara canis*
- *Echinococcus granulosus*
- *Chlamydia psittaci*
- *Campylobacter spp*

NOTE – This is by no means a definitive list, nor is it intended to imply that all Jack Russell terriers carry these diseases.

In order to minimise the risk of contracting any of these diseases, all pet owners should take care to practise good hygiene routines at all times, and particularly when they have been handling their terriers or working them on wild animals.

These precautions could be described as common sense, and should include the following:

Even a scruffy carry box like this one will offer security and safety to both the JRs and their owner who shares the car.

- Always wash your hands after handling any animal, including your JR.
- Always wash your hands after handling any wild animal, or spending time hunting, digging etc. in the area where wild animals will be.
- Never allow your JR to lick your (or anyone else's) face.
- Use only dog dishes and utensils kept solely for the use of dogs. Never allow any dog to eat or drink from human cups, plates etc.
- All washing of dogs' dishes and other such utensils should, wherever possible, be carried out in areas specifically intended for such a purpose. If you have to use the same sink as the family's washing, ensure that the sink and all surrounding areas are thoroughly disinfected after such use. Rather than use the family sink, I would recommend that you use a bucket and/or bowl which is specifically for the JRs in your family.
- All food preparation should be carried out well away from the human food preparation area, preferably in areas only used for this purpose. Never use knives etc. for both human food preparation and the preparation of food for your JR.
- Remove all faeces from kennels, runs etc. as soon as possible. This waste must then be disposed of in a proper and safe fashion.
- Do not hesitate to seek medical advice if you suspect that you may have contracted or been exposed to any zoonotic disease.

Vaccinations

Puppies are born with their own immune system, acquired from the bitch. However, this immunity will last for only twelve weeks maximum. In order to safeguard our JRs, we should have them vaccinated and given boosters every twelve months.

Diseases for which your puppy should be vaccinated vary from country to country around the world, but in the UK, your JR, as a puppy, should be vaccinated against the following diseases, and given yearly boosters, as advised by your veterinary surgeon. Without regular boosters, your JR will not have the immunity to fight off these diseases, and so it is vital that you keep all of your dogs up to date with their vaccinations, in order to minimise any risk from these diseases.

- Canine distemper
- Infectious canine hepatitis
- Canine leptospirosis
- Canine parvovirus
- Contagious respiratory disease

Veterinary recommendations on when puppies should be vaccinated for various diseases vary, not least of all due to on-going research. In addition, the type of vaccine used will also affect the timings. It is recommended that you seek the advice of your own veterinary surgeon well before you purchase a puppy or breed from your bitch. Until such time as your puppy is fully vaccinated, and given the 'all clear' by your veterinary surgeon, he should not be taken out in any public space, nor allowed to come into contact with any dog that you are not certain is fully vaccinated and free from disease.

CHAPTER 8

THE LAW

Whatever we do, we are all of us subject to the laws of the land in which we live. Many of these laws have no real direct link with dogs, such as the laws on theft, and yet they can still apply to dogs. Neither is ignorance any excuse, and so it benefits all of us if we have a working understanding of the laws which will affect us and our actions. Unfortunately, just to complicate matters even further, laws change, seemingly all too frequently at times.

In this chapter, I intend to outline the main Acts of Parliament (laws) which affect JR owners in England and Wales. Unfortunately, even in such a confined area, differences will still apply, as the laws in England and Wales often differ from those in Scotland. All of these factors should be considered when reading this chapter.

While I have endeavoured to give accurate details and interpretations on the laws covered, the following is in no way intended to be a definitive guide to the law, and neither the author nor the publisher can accept any liability for any omission or mistake contained in this book.

The acts are listed in alphabetical order only.

The Abandonment of Animals Act, 1960

If any person abandons their Jack Russell, or any other animal, without reasonable excuse and in circumstances where it is reasonable to assume that the animal would suffer, they are guilty of an offence under this Act. Such abandonment is also an offence of cruelty within the meaning of the Protection of Animals Act, 1911.

The Animals' Boarding Establishments Act, 1963

It is unlawful for any person to keeping a boarding establishment for cats and/or dogs, unless they hold a licence, as defined within this act. The licences are issued by the local authority in whose area the establishment lies.

All such boarding establishments have to adhere to and comply with rules and regulations concerning the size and construction of the establishment, and the disposal of waste materials, among other regulations. All of these rules and regulations are covered within the local authority's 'standard licence conditions'.

The Animals Act, 1971

If your Jack Russell causes damage to another person's property, for example by running onto a road, causing a driver to swerve to avoid hitting him and, in so doing, the driver's car and/or other property is damaged, you, as owner of the dog, are responsible for the financial implications.

These financial implications may be with regard to actual damage of property such as a car, a fence, a building etc., but may also be the damage to humans and/or animals. If the driver of the accident just described loses his income for a period as a direct result of the accident caused by your Jack Russell, he may well sue you for loss of earnings, as well as physical pain etc. Similarly, a farmer can sue you for damages if, for example, your Jack Russell 'worries' sheep or other livestock.

The Breeding of Dogs Act, 1973

Only those who hold a licence granted under this Act may run a dog breeding establishment. The licences are granted by the local authority, and they will impose restrictions on the manner in which the dogs are kept and housed, and also on items such as the disposal of waste materials etc.

Under this Act, the term 'breeding establishment' means any premises where two or more bitches are kept for the purpose of breeding dogs for sale.

The Dangerous Dogs Act, 1991

Although most people know that this Act outlaws the keeping of certain breeds (i.e. the 'Dogo Argentino', the 'Fila Brasileiro' and any other breed 'being types appearing to be bred for fighting or having the characteristics of types bred for that purpose'), and the registration and neutering of 'pit bull terrier types of dog', it should be remembered that parts of this Act apply to every breed of dog, including mongrels and cross-breeds etc.

Under this Act it is unlawful to have a dog 'dangerously out of control' in a public place. A dog is deemed to be 'dangerously out of control' on any occasion when there are grounds for reasonable apprehension that it would injure any person, whether or not it actually does so. In any successful prosecution, the dog would have to be destroyed. The term 'public place', is defined as any street, road or other place to which the public have, or are permitted to have, access.

The Dogs (Protection of Livestock) Act, 1953

Under this Act, the owner and/or handler of a Jack Russell or any other breed of dog which 'worries' livestock on agricultural land is guilty of an offence.

The term 'worrying' is defined as 'a dog attacking or chasing livestock so that injury or suffering is likely', or 'not being on a lead or under close control in an enclosure in which there are sheep'. Of interest to readers will be that, where sheep are in an enclosure, a trained sheep dog, gundog or pack of hounds being in that enclosure with the sheep does not constitute an offence.

The Guard Dog Act, 1975
Under this Act, if you were to use your Jack Russell to 'protect premises, or property kept on premises', the JR would, in the eyes of the law, be a guard dog. As such, you must display a suitable warning sign at each entrance to the premises which the JR is guarding. In addition, the JR must either be accompanied by a handler, or fastened to prevent its wandering the premises.

The Performing Animals (Regulation) Act, 1925
This Act deals with the exhibition and training of 'performing animals'; it does not cover invertebrate species.

Under this Act, it is unlawful for anyone to train any animal to perform, unless that person is registered with their local authority. The term 'exhibit' is defined in the Act as 'exhibit at any entertainment to which the public are admitted, whether on payment or otherwise' and 'train' is defined as 'train for the purpose of any such exhibition'.

The Act does not apply to the training of any animals for bona fide military, police, agricultural or sporting purposes, or the exhibition of any such trained animals.

Under this Act, neither trainers who show dogs in a competition nor those who organise and/or train dogs for terrier racing need to register for licensing. All registrations and licensing are carried out by the local authority in whose area the training establishment is situated.

The Pests Act, 1954
Under this Act, the occupier of any land must do all they can to control the number of rabbits on that land. This is a useful Act for those who wish to obtain areas on which to work their terriers on rabbits.

The Pet Animals Act, 1951
This Act deals with the sale of pet animals as a business, i.e. a 'pet shop'. Under this Act, it is an offence to run such a business without holding the relevant licence, issued by the local authority. The Act imposes restrictions and duties on the holder of the licence to ensure the health and welfare of the animals within his 'shop'. The Act also makes it unlawful to sell any animal to children under the age of twelve years, and it is also unlawful to run a 'pet shop' selling animals in the street.

It should be noted that this Act will not apply to most keepers and breeders of Jack Russell terriers, since the Act specifically excludes from the need to hold such a licence, 'the keeping or selling of pedigree animals that a person has bred, or the offspring of an animal kept by him as a pet'. Also, if you were to buy in other JRs, for either show, breeding or working purposes, and then decide that you wanted to sell any or all of these terriers, that is also allowed under the Act, and no licence is required.

Readers should also note that the term 'pedigree animal' does not simply refer to Parson Jack Russell terriers registered with the Kennel Club, as the Act defines pedigree animals as 'an animal of any description which is by its breeding, eligible for registration with a recognised club or society keeping a register of animals of that description'.

The Protection of Animals Act, 1911
This is the most important piece of legislation affecting the keeping of Jack Russell terriers and other animals, in England and Wales. In general, this Act makes it unlawful to be 'cruel' to any captive or domesticated animal. Note, therefore, that it does not cover wild animals (unless they are made captive, at which time they are covered by this Act).

The cruelty may be physical, in the form of kicking, torturing, or baiting, or it may mean lack of care, such as not feeding an animal, not housing it correctly, or not giving it medical care and treatment if and when the animal requires such treatment. In addition, the cruelty can also be psychological, for example it is unlawful under this Act to deliberately put a live rat in an enclosure with a terrier. Dog fighting is specifically unlawful under this Act.

The Protection of Animals (Anaesthetics) Act, 1954
This Act forbids any operation on a JR without the use of anaesthetics. Exemptions from this rule include first aid or similar actions which are designed to save the animal's life or lessen pain, amputation of the JR's dew claws before the terrier's eyes are open, and any other minor operation usually performed without anaesthetic by a veterinary surgeon because of its quickness and painlessness.

The Road Traffic Act, 1972
This Act carries a section which makes it an offence to have a dog which is not under the control of the owner/handler when that dog is on a highway (road).

The Veterinary Surgeons Act, 1966
This is the Act which was amended so that only qualified veterinary surgeons may dock a dog's tail. Prior to that amendment, any person over the age of

eighteen was allowed to dock the tails of their dogs, providing that this action was carried out before the puppy's eyes had opened. At this age, according to the veterinary surgeons of a few years ago, docking of tails was considered a 'minor operation usually performed without anaesthetic by a veterinary surgeon because of its quickness and painlessness'.

The Wild Mammals Protection Act, 1996

Under this Act, it is an offence to deliberately inflict pain and suffering on any wild mammal. Where an act of killing any wild mammal can be shown to have been carried out on an animal that was so seriously disabled due to the actions of others or as a consequence of an accident, and so had no reasonable chance of recovery, the person(s) concerned cannot have committed any offence under this Act.

The Act prohibits any person from deliberately mutilating, kicking, beating nailing, impaling, stabbing, burning, stoning, crushing, drowning, dragging or asphyxiating any wild mammal with intent to inflict unnecessary suffering.

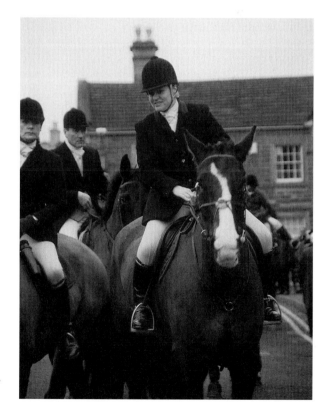

Members of a Derbyshire hunt prepare to start a day's sport. Good terriers are indispensable to hunts like this.

Properly conducted terrier work will not fall into any of these categories, and the intention of this Act is not to interfere with work of this nature, which all fair-minded people will accept as legitimate and necessary. The Act was passed to stop those individuals who, for reasons best known to themselves, deliberately inflict pain and suffering on wild mammals.

The Wildlife and Countryside Act

This Act bestows varying levels of protection on the fauna and flora of the country, making some 'pest' species which can be 'taken' by any authorised persons, while others are totally protected. Under this Act, foxes are pests, allowed to be taken by authorised people at any time, while badgers are 'fully protected', and it is an offence to even disturb their sett, the underground home of the badger. Because of this, great care must be taken when out walking your Jack Russell, as all terriers are drawn to burrows, regardless of any legal aspect concerned with their actions. If your JR should venture on or into a badger sett, it will be extremely difficult to prove that this was accidental, and you may well find yourself facing charges of badger digging or some similar felony. It is best to give a very wide berth to all badger setts, although if you are in an area unknown to yourself, it will be almost impossible to do this.

TERRIER TERMS

Account for   a hunting term meaning to kill or run the fox to ground.

All on   a hunting term used by the hunt's whipper-in, meaning that all of the pack's hounds are present.

Autosomes   chromosomes other than those which determine the sex of the progeny of a mating.

Benching   the act of placing terriers on the show bench, for the attention of the judge officiating at that show.

Billett   a fox's droppings.

Bitch   a female Jack Russell or any other breed of dog.

Bolt   a hunting term meaning to drive out a fox from a subterranean refuge, usually using a terrier.

Brush   the fox's tail.

Canines   the front teeth of a dog, which in the wild it would use to kill its prey.

Carbohydrates   food constituents which provide the body with energy and material for growth.

Cast   a term used in the hunting field for the efforts made by hounds to find a lost fox's scent.

Charlie
Charles Edward } country names for the fox.

Chromosomes   thread-like bodies, carried inside the nucleus of every germ cell, which carry the genes of the individual animal.

Classes   at a dog show, entries are divided into classes, to facilitate judging. These classes are usually dictated by colour, age, coat type or sex of the Jack Russell concerned.

Coitus   the physical act of mating.

Collar   usually a leather or nylon collar used to keep control of Jack Russells while on a lead. The term is also used to denote the collar onto which is attached the transmitter used for tracking terriers while they are working underground; this is sometimes referred to as 'an electronic collar'.

Cope   a metal muzzle.
   See also 'muzzle'.

Crepuscular the term used to describe an animal that is active around the hours of dusk and dawn.

Cub a young fox.

Culling the deliberate removal and killing of some or all of the pups in a litter which is thought to be too large for the mother to rear. I believe this to be unnecessary, as the bitch will know her own limits, culling the litter as she sees fit, starting with the weakest members. Where deformed or injured puppies are concerned, however, the culling of these individuals is to be recommended.

Dam The mother of a litter.

Diurnal active in the day, resting at night.

Dog the male Jack Russell or any other breed of dog, or the animal itself, i.e. *Canis familiaris*.

Dominant a gene which will always show itself in the phenotype of a JR, even if there is only one of these genes present. Such genes are denoted by the use of an upper case (capital) letter.

Dystocia a bitch's inability to give birth.

Earth the fox's underground home.

Ectoparasite a parasite which lives on the outside of the host animal e.g. fleas, lice and ticks.
> See also 'Parasite' and Endoparasite'.

Electronic detector a device for tracking terriers while they are working underground. The device consists of a collar-mounted transmitter (worn by the terrier) and a hand-held receiver. Both are pre-tuned. A modern detector can be used to a depth of up to five metres (fifteen feet).

Endoparasite a parasite that lives inside the host animal, (e.g. in the intestines etc.), such as tapeworms.
> See also 'Parasite' and Ectoparasite'.

Enter to get a terrier working, usually a terrier is said to have been entered when he has made his first catch or kill.

Fats constituents of food which provide the terrier's body with energy. A surplus of fats in a JR's diet will cause it to become overweight, and endanger its health, particularly if the terrier is also deprived of sufficient exercise. Fats contain about two and a half times as much energy (gram for gram) as carbohydrates.

Fibre the indigestible material present in some foods which helps stimulate the action of the intestines. Used to be known as 'Roughage'.

Gene a hereditary factor of inherited material. Genes are carried on the chromosome.

Genetics the study of the ways in which certain characteristics are passed on from one generation to the next.

Genitals (Genitalia) the external sex organs of the Jack Russell.

Genotype   the genetic make-up of the Jack Russell.

Genus   a group of animals containing species which closely resemble each other, e.g. dogs and wolves (the Canidae).

Germ cell   the egg of a bitch, and the sperm of the male terrier.

Gestation   pregnancy. The bitch's gestation period (pregnancy) is often quoted as being exactly 63 days. It can, in fact, last between 54–72 days, with the average being 60 days. This is the actual time between fertilisation and whelping.

Hackles   the hairs down the ridge of a JR's neck and spine.

Heat   a term often used to describe oestrus.

Heat-stroke   the effect of too much heat on a terrier. If this condition is not treated, it can be fatal. Sometimes referred to as 'the sweats'.

Hernia   a protrusion of part of the dog's organs through an abnormal opening in the surrounding tissues.

Hybrid   a crossbred animal, i.e. heterozygous. The term is sometimes used to denote the progeny of a mating of a closely bred animal and a completely unrelated one (a crossbreed) or the mating of a Jack Russell with another variety of dog, e.g. a Lakeland terrier.

Hybrid vigour   the increased vigour and resistance to disease often found in the offspring resulting from the mating of completely unrelated dogs. The author believes the benefits of so-called hybrid vigour are much overstated. The advocates of hybrid vigour will tell listeners that mongrel dogs are far less susceptible to disease and illness than are pure-bred dogs, which is nonsense.

Inbreeding   the practice of breeding very closely related Jack Russells together. *See also* 'line-breeding'.

Incinerator   a device for burning rubbish (especially faeces, soiled shavings and bedding). Essential for the safe disposal of bedding and shavings etc. of infected and ill terriers.

Incisors   the front teeth of a terrier.

Inheritance   the manner in which certain characteristics are passed from one generation to the next.

Intractability   lack of tameness; impossible to handle without the risk of being bitten.

Life expectancy   *see* 'Longevity'.

Line   a 'family' of Jack Russells, bred for several generations.

Line-breeding   a moderated form of inbreeding, i.e. using related animals other than those from the close family.

Litter   the puppies produced at one whelping.

Lochia   the greenish fluid vaginal discharge about 24 hours after a bitch has whelped.

Locus   position on a chromosome occupied by a specific gene (plural *locii*).

Longevity   length of life. In the Jack Russell, this is about 12–14 years, although some would argue about the quality of life of an elderly Jack Russell terrier.

Marking   the action of a terrier at the mouth of a fox's earth or rabbit's burrow, telling the owner and the rest of the pack that the terrier has found someone at home.

Mask   a fox's head.

Mating   *see* 'Coitus'.

Minerals   minute constituents of a terrier's diet, without which he will not have a balanced diet, with a consequent adverse effect on his health.

Monohybrid inheritance   the inheritance of a single characteristic.

Mutant   the changed gene which results in a change in an animal; more accurately known as a mutant allele.

Muzzle   a device for preventing the terrier from biting (either humans or his natural quarry). Can be made from leather, string, plastic, nylon or even metal. Also the name for the Jack Russell's nose.

Myxomatosis   a deadly viral disease amongst rabbits. Thought to have been deliberately introduced to the UK from France, to 'control' the numbers of wild rabbits.

Nocturnal   the term used to describe an animal that is active by night, sleeping by day.

Oestrus   the state in which a bitch will accept a mating. *See also* 'Heat'.

Oestrus Cycle   the sexual cycle of a bitch.

Overshot   a jaw whose upper incisors overlap those on the bottom jaw.

Ovulation   the release of eggs into the womb of the bitch to be fertilised by the dog's sperm.

Oxytocin   a hormone, often given in an injection to help ensure that the uterus contracts down properly, and expels all of its contents.

Pad   a fox's foot.

Parasites   animals which live on or in other animals (hosts) in a manner which is detrimental to the host. Includes worms, fleas, mites, lice and ticks. *See also* 'endoparasites' and 'ectoparasites'.

Paunch   (v) to remove the 'guts' of a rabbit.
   (n) an animal's stomach.

Pen   an old-fashioned term for a kennel.

Phenotype   the physical appearance of the Jack Russell.

Photoperiodism   the dependence on the daytime/night-time (or simply light and dark) ratio of various biological functions, particularly the commencement of oestrus in Jack Russells and many other species of animal.

Polecat   the common name of the animal *Mustela putorius*. Strictly, this name should only be used to describe the wild polecat, but today it is also commonly used to describe any domesticated ferret with polecat-type markings. The name originates from the French *Poulet Chat* – chicken cat.

Poley   a domesticated ferret with the typical wild polecat markings.

Pregnancy   *see* 'Gestation'.

Proteins   the basic constituents of all living things, which are an essential component of a balanced diet, essential for growth and tissue maintenance. Puppies, young dogs, bitches during pregnancy and while lactating all require extra proteins, as do hard-working dogs and those used for stud purposes.

Recessive   a gene which is masked unless another identical gene is present in a terrier. Such genes are denoted by writing their code in lower case letters.

Records   all of the information concerning your Jack Russell. These records must always be kept accurately.

Roughage   an old-fashioned term for fibre.

Scissor bite   where the upper teeth closely overlap the lower teeth and are set square to the jaws. This is this ideal for all Jack Russell terriers.

Scours   diarrhoea.

Season   *see* 'Oestrus'.

Sett   the underground home of the badger (*Meles meles*).

Sex chromosomes   the chromosomes responsible for determining the sex of a terrier. Males have one X chromosome and one Y. Females have a pair of X chromosomes. All other chromosomes are known as autosomes.

Sex-linked   the term used to describe a characteristic where the mutant inheritance allele is carried on the sex chromosome and is, therefore, governed by the sex of the individual.

Sexual dimorphism   the differences exhibited between the sexes e.g. the male Jack Russell always has the capacity to grow larger than the bitch.

Sibling   brother or sister; litter mate.

Sire   the father of a litter.

Skulk   when a terrier refuses to leave the mouth of a tunnel, it is said to be 'skulking'.

Speak   to give tongue, bark etc.

Sport   the term used to indicate a terrier that is genetically different from the norm.

Stud   an individual Jack Russell breeder's kennel, where JRs are bred. Some clubs allow one to register a stud prefix (name) which is exclusive to the registrant. Often used to describe the male Jack Russell used for breeding purposes.

Stud book   the record (not necessarily a book) of all of the terriers in a particular stud.

Sweats   see 'Heat-stroke'.

Terrier detector or locator   see 'Electronic detector'.

Undershot   a jaw whose lower incisors overlap those on the top jaw.

Variety   a specific colour and coat type of the Jack Russell, e.g. smooth-coated, tan-and-white.

Vaccination   an injection of a mild form of a specific pathogenic micro-organism, which causes the body to form antibodies, thus helping to prevent the treated animal from acquiring a full dose of the specific disease, e.g. distemper.

Virus   an organism able to cause disease.

Vitamin deficiency   the lack of certain important vitamins; this term is usually used to indicate the result of such a deficiency, rather than the actual lack of the vitamin(s) in question.

Vitamins   organic compounds, essential to the health of a terrier. Usually referred to by letters of the alphabet, e.g. A, B, C, etc.

Vixen   a female fox.

Weaning   the development of the eating habits of terrier puppies when they progress from being dependent upon their mothers for food, and are capable of feeding themselves, i.e. eating solid food.

Whelping   the act of a bitch giving birth.

Whelps   unweaned puppies.

Zoonoses   diseases capable of being transmitted from an animal species to humans, e.g. salmonellosis.

Zoonotic disease   a disease which is capable of being transmitted from an animal to humans.

Zygote   a fertilised egg.

BIBLIOGRAPHY

Alsoton, George G, with Vanacore, Connie – *The Winning Edge – Show Ring Secrets*. Howell Books, New York, 1992

Council for Nature – *Predatory Mammals in Britain*. Council for Nature, 1967

Crofts, Wendy – *A Summary of the Statute Law Relating to Animal Welfare in England and Wales*. Universities Federation for Animal Welfare, revised 1986

Davies, EM – *Memoirs of The Reverend John Russell and His Outdoor Life*. Chatto and Windus, 1878

Dunbar, Dr Ian – *Dog Behaviour – Why dogs do what they do*. TFH Publications, 1979

Edney, Andrew – *The Waltham Book of Dog and Cat Nutrition*. Pergamon Press, 1982

Edney, Andrew, with Mugford, Dr Roger – *Dog and Puppy Care – A Practical Guide*. Salamander Books, 1987

Evans, Jim – *Breeding from Your Bitch – A guide for owners*. Pedigree Petfoods, 1994

Evans, Jim and White, Kay – *The Book of the Bitch*. Henston, 1988

Evans, Jim and White, Kay – *The Doglopaedia*. Siebert Publications, 1987

Fiennes, Richard and Alice – *The Natural History of the Dog*. Weidenfeld and Nicolson, 1968

Head, Ann – *Good Dog! Educating the family pet*. Popular Dogs, 1987

Hobson, Jeremy – *Working Terriers – Management and Training*. The Crowood Press, 1987

Horner, Tom – *Terriers of the World – their history and characteristics*. Faber, 1984

Jackson, Frank – *Cruft's – the official HISTORY*. Pelham Books, London, 1990

Jackson, Frank – *Dog Breeding – the Theory and the Practice*. The Crowood Press, 1994

Jackson, Jean and Frank – *The Making of the Parson Jack Russell terrier*. Boydell and Brewer, 1986

Jackson, Jean and Frank – *Parson Jack Russell Terriers.* The Crowood Press, 1990

Jackson, Jean and Frank – *The Parson and Jack Russell Terriers.* Popular Dogs, 1991

Lawrence, MJ and Brown, RW – *Mammals of Britain – Their tracks, trails and signs.* Blandford Press, 1973

Lucas, Sir Jocelyn – *Hunt and Working Terriers.* Chapman and Hall, 1931

MacDonald, David (Editor) – *The Complete Book of the Dog.* Pelham Books, 1985

McKay, James – *The Ferret and Ferreting Handbook.* The Crowood Press, 1987

McKay, James – *The Complete Guide to Ferrets.* Swan Hill Press, 1994

Morris, Dr Desmond – *Dog Watching.* Jonathan Cape, 1986.

O'Farrell, Valerie – *Manual of Canine Behaviour.* British Small Animal Veterinary Association, 1976

Palmer, Joan – *Training Your Dog.* Salamander, 1987

Plummer, D Brian – *The Complete Jack Russell Terrier.* The Boydell Press, 1980

Plummer, D Brian – *Tales of a Rat Hunting Man.* The Boydell Press, 1978

Plummer, D Brian – *The Working Terrier.* Boydell and Brewer, 1978

Robinson, Roy – *Genetics for Dog Breeders.* Pergamon Press, 1982

Ruiz, Suzanne – *Grooming Your Dog.* Salamander Books, 1987

Russell, Dan – *Jack Russell and his Terriers.* Jack Russell Terrier Club of Great Britain, 1999

Sandys-Winsch, Godfrey – *Your Dog and the Law.* Shaw and Sons, 1978

Scanziani, Piero – *The British Encyclopaedia of Dogs.* Orbis, 1981

Silvernail, Evelyn R – *The New Complete Fox Terrier.* Howell, 1976

Smythe, RH – *The Breeding and Rearing of Dogs.* Popular Dogs, 1969

Sutton, Catherine G – *Dog Shows and Show Dogs* – a definitive Study. K and R Classics Books, Horncastle, England, 1980

Sylvester, Patricia (Editor) – *The Reader's Digest Illustrated Book of Dogs.* The Reader's Digest, 1982

Taylor, David – *You and Your Dog.* Dorling Kindersley, 1986

Taylor, David – *The Ultimate Dog Book.* Dorling Kindersley, 1990

Thorne, Chris J (Editor) – *The Waltham Book of Dog and Cat Behaviour.* Pergamon Press, 1992.

Tucker, Michael – *Solving Your Dog Problems – A practical handbook for owners and trainers.* Robert Hale, London, 1987

Turner, Trevor – *Veterinary Notes for Dog Owners.* Popular Dogs, 1980.

Williams, Elsie – *Fox Terrier.* Popular Dogs, 1965

USEFUL ORGANISATIONS AND CONTACTS

Listed below are the contact addresses of some useful organisations. Please ensure that you enclose a self-addressed stamped envelope with all enquiries. As many telephone numbers are set to change in the near future, I have deliberately omitted them from this list; directory enquiries will be able to give you the correct number from the details provided in this list.

The inclusion of any organisation should not be seen as any kind of endorsement for that organisation from the author, and neither should the omission of any organisation be seen as any form of disapproval of that organisation by the author.

Where the organisation has only voluntary officers, readers must remember that these officials – and therefore the contact name and address – will change from time to time.

The British Association for Shooting and Conservation (BASC), UK Headquarters, Marford Mill, Rossett, Wrexham, Clwyd LL12 OHL.

The representative body for sporting shooting in the United Kingdom. The Association has Regional Offices in many parts of the UK, including Northern Ireland. Membership of the BASC confers insurance cover essential for participation in any country sport including the working of terriers on legitimate quarry.

The Council of Docked Breeds, Marsburg Kennels, Whitehall Lane, Thorpe-le-Soken, Essex CO16 OAF.

The Council's objectives are the safeguarding of traditionally docked breeds and defending the tail-docking option. Members are given help, advice and assistance on all aspects of tail docking of puppies. Where a member may have difficulty finding a veterinary surgeon willing to dock the tails of Jack Russell puppies, the Council may well be able to put that member in touch with a veterinary surgeon who will help.

The Country Landowners' Association, 16 Belgrave Square, London SWIX 8PQ.

The Countryman's Weekly, Yelverton, Devon PL20 7PE
A weekly magazine featuring terrier work, shows etc., as well as other legitimate country sports.

The Countryside Alliance, The Old Town Hall, 367 Kennington Road, London SF11 4PT.
The Alliance promotes country sports and the wider concerns of country people. The Countryside Alliance, among many other positive actions, organised the rallies and marches which have put country sports and the countryside in general back in the minds of the government, and presented an entirely positive image. Everyone who feels strongly about the continuance of legitimate country sports, and who really cares for the British countryside, and the flora and fauna therein, should be a member of the Alliance. The Alliance will help members seeking opportunities to work their Jack Russells.

Deben Group Industries Ltd, Deben Way, Melton, Woodbridge, Suffolk IP12 IRS.
Manufacturers of electronic terrier detectors, etc.

The Farming and Wildlife Advisory Group (FWAG), Sparsholt College, Sparsholt, Winchester S021 2LD.
FWAG offers practical, cost effective environmental advice for commercial farmers and landowners.

The Field, Room 2107, Kings Reach Tower, Stamford Street, London SE1 9LS.
A monthly magazine which often features articles on hunting and other country sports.

The Game Conservancy Trust, Burgate Manor, Fordingbridge, Hampshire 5P6 1FF.
A unique advisory and research organisation for game habitat management.

The Jack Russell Terrier Club of Great Britain (JRTCGB), c/o Brian Male, Tyke's Farm, Somerley Lane, Earnley, Chichester, West Sussex PO20 7JB.

Lintran, 1 Hawthorn Road, Cherry Willingham, Lincoln LN3 4JU.
Manufacturers of top quality dog and transit equipment.

The Ministry of Agriculture, Fisheries and Food, Whitehall Place, London.

The National Ferret School, PO Box 61, Chesterfield, Derbyshire S45 015. e-mail Enquiries@Honeybank.co.uk

An organisation established by the author, which runs courses covering all aspects of ferrets and ferreting, including the use of terriers, gundog breeds and hawks to control the rabbit population. The School also sells equipment, books and videos relating to course activities.

The Parson Jack Russell Terrier Club, c/o Mrs M Evans, Preseli Filling Station, Llanddewi Velfrey, Narberth, Pembrokeshire.

The Royal Society for the Prevention of Cruelty to Animals. Fighting all cruelty to animals.

The Shooting Gazette, BPG (Bourne) Ltd, 2 West Street, Bourne, Lincolnshire PE10 9NE.

A monthly magazine for country sports enthusiasts.

Shooting Times and Country magazine, Room 2-08, Kings Reach Tower, Stamford Street, London SEI 9LS.

A weekly magazine featuring shooting, terrier work, etc.

Sporting Gun magazine, Kings Reach Tower, Stamford Street, London SEI 9LS.

A monthly magazine featuring many country sports, including working terriers.

James Wellbeloved and Co. Ltd, Yeovil, Somerset BA20 2JB.

Manufacturers of top quality dog, cat and ferret foods.

THE NEW QUARANTINE LAWS FOR THE UK

Until very recently, the United Kingdom had extremely stringent laws concerning the quarantining of animals entering the country. With very few exceptions, all animals had to spend six months in an approved quarantine centre. This system has been so effective that Britain has seen very few minor outbreaks and no major outbreaks of rabies since its inception.

The system and the quarantine centres have been so highly regarded around the world that several countries, such as Australia, insist that animals from a third country must spend six months in a UK quarantine centre before going to that country, and then only serve a minimal time in quarantine in the new home country. Recently, however, the UK Government has seen fit to alter the rules and regulations governing quarantine, and it is not yet known whether these new rules will keep rabies at bay as effectively as the old rules did. Neither is it clear whether Australia and other countries who have used our quarantine system to ensure that rabies is kept out of their country, will continue to do so.

Following the outline announcement by the UK Government on 26 March, 1999, full details of the new 'Pet Travel Scheme' (to be known as 'PETS') were announced by Baroness Hayman, Minister of State at MAFF, in August, 1999. Baroness Hayman said that the new Travel Scheme will largely replace the existing quarantine system. It is hoped that a pilot scheme will be fully in place by April 2000 but the first pets may be able to come into the UK, under this new system, early in 2000. The final scheme will be in place by April 2001.

The UK Government claims to have listened to the views of pet owners and others before it decided not to restrict the pilot scheme to longer-stay travellers, and it is hoped that the pilot scheme will be a wide-ranging test of what will happen under the main scheme. All the transport companies which want to take part will do so, and the pilot will cover the routes they have chosen.

In launching the new scheme, Baroness Hayman expressed her delight at the 'modernising' of the quarantine system, and stated that the new arrangements will keep Britain fully protected against rabies while letting pet owners take their cat or dog abroad. She said that cat and dog owners would now be able to take steps to prepare for the new pilot scheme that would allow them to travel to and from countries in Western Europe, without the need to leave their family pets at home, or their having to 'endure' six months in quarantine.

In addition, the Baroness said that dogs providing assistance to the disabled, including guide and hearing dogs, may be able to travel by air between the UK and Australia and New Zealand.

Under the new scheme, pet owners who wish to qualify must:

1. get their pets microchipped.
2. vaccinate their pets against rabies.
3. ensure their pets have undertaken a blood test from a MAFF-recognised laboratory, in order to confirm that the vaccine has taken.

A wide range of routes to the United Kingdom will be tested, and these will include the Calais to Dover sea routes, Shuttle services in the Channel Tunnel, certain sea routes into Portsmouth from Normandy and Brittany and air routes into Heathrow from Europe. The companies who will be running such routes

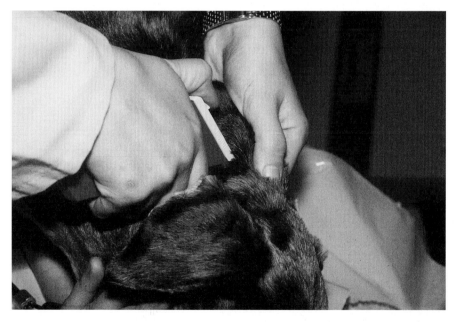

An Identichip being inserted in a dog's neck, just under the skin. Such operations are virtually painless, but the chip offers high security, and is essential if a dog is to travel abroad.

must satisfy the Government that they have the necessary systems in place to check every pet they carry. Once authorised by the Government, these companies will be subject to regular audit and inspection to ensure standards are being maintained. There will also be spot checks on animals, as they enter the UK, carried out by MAFF officials.

The first step for any reader who may wish to take advantage of this scheme, is to arrange the microchipping of their animal(s), to give permanent proof of their identity. Veterinary surgeons and others will be able to advise you on this matter, and also to carry out the implant. Transport companies will be able to read all microchips which meet the norms of the International Standards Organisation, which all microchip implants in the UK will. If for any reason the microchip used does not conform to these standards, and the normal scanners are unable to read the chip's information, the owner will need to supply a suitable reader which is able to read it.

The vaccination against rabies must take place after the microchipping, in order to guarantee the identity of the animal. Even if a pet has previously been vaccinated but not microchipped, it will have to receive a microchip and subsequently be revaccinated.

Owners should then arrange for a blood sample to be taken by their vet approximately 30 days after vaccination to ensure that it has taken. The

The Identichip information being read, using a scanner in a vet's surgery.

sample can only be tested at recognised laboratories. MAFF has so far recognised eleven laboratories including the Veterinary Laboratory Agency in Weybridge. The names of further laboratories will be announced as and when approval is granted. Blood test results will only be accepted under PETS if the test was carried out on or after 27 May 1999, the date of acceptance.

The recognised laboratories have limited capacity at the moment. Pet owners should therefore check with their vet, before having their pet vaccinated, to find out how long the wait will be for a blood test. Should there be a long wait it may be wise to delay vaccination, because the best test results come about 30 days after vaccination.

Pets in the UK and Ireland that gave a blood sample before the pilot scheme started may go abroad and come back into this country once the blood test is satisfactory. Pets which give a blood sample later, or which are resident outside the UK or Ireland will have to wait six months after a successful blood test result before they can come into the UK.

To show that the pets meet the microchipping, vaccination and blood test requirements, the owner must obtain a certificate from a vet authorised by the Government in the country concerned. This certificate will be available, closer to the start of the pilot.

The final procedure is for the pet to be treated for tapeworm and ticks between 24 and 48 hours before returning to the UK. This is to prevent the spreading of tapeworms and ticks to humans from wildlife outside the UK as identified by the Kennedy Committee. This treatment must also be certified by a vet authorised by the Government from the country concerned. Under this scheme cats and dogs from Canada and the United States are not eligible due to the occurrence of rabies in North American wildlife, but the issue of including these countries will be returned to after the main scheme has started in 2001.

At present pets may move freely within the British Isles (the UK, Channel Isles, Isle of Man and the Republic of Ireland) without any need for microchipping or vaccination. This will continue as long as pets do not go outside of the British Isles.

Consultation on the statutory instrument to give effect to the pilot scheme will start shortly.

The laboratories recognised by MAFF for carrying out blood tests under the Pet Travel Scheme are:

Veterinary Laboratory Agency
New Haw, Addlestone
Surrey KT15 3NB
UNITED KINGDOM Tel: (+44) 01932 357 345
Fax: (+44) 01932 357 856

Agence Française De Securite Sanitaire des Aliments
Nancy
Domaine de Pixerecourt
B.P. 9 F-54220
Malzéville
FRANCE Tel: (+33) 3 83 29 89 50
Fax: (+33) 3 83 29 89 59

National Vetinary Institute
Commision of Diagnostics
Section of Diagnostics
Department of Virology
PO Box 585
BMCS-751 23 Uppsala
SWEDEN Tel:(+ 46) 1867 4000
Fax:(+ 46) 184714517

Danish Veterinary Institute for Virus Research
Lindholm
DK-4771 Kalvehave
DENMARK Tel: (+45) 55 86 02 00
Fax: (+45) 55 86 03 00

National Veterinary and Food Research Institute
PL 368 (Heimeentie 57)
00231 Helsinki
FINLAND Tel: (+35) 89 393 1901
Fax: (+35) 89 393 1811

Instut für Virologie
Frankfurter Strasse 107
D – 35392 Giessen
GERMANY Tel: (+49) 641 99 38350
Fax: (+49) 641 99 38359

Dept. for Equine, Pets and Vaccine Control Virology Unit
Federal Institute for the Control of Viral Infection in Animals
Robert Kochgasse 17
2340 Mödling
AUSTRIA Tel: (+43) 2236 46 640 902 or 906
Fax: (+43) 2236 46 640 941

Instituto Zooprofilattico Sperimentale delle Venezie
Via Romea 14/A
I-35020 Legonaro (PD)
ITALY Tel: (+39) 049 80 70 306
Fax: (+39) 049 88 30 046

Direccion General de Sanidad de la Produccion Agaria
Laboratorio de Sanidad y Produccion Animal del Estado
Camino del Jau, S/N
E-18320 Santa Fé (Granada)
SPAIN Tel: (+34) 958 44 03 75
Fax: (+34) 958 44 12 00

Institute Pasteur of Brussels
Rue Engeland 642
B-1180 Brussels
BELGIUM Tel: (+32) 2 373 31 58
Fax: (+32) 2 373 31 74

Institute of Veterinary Virology
Schweizerische Tollwutzentrale
Langgass-Strasse 122
CH-3012 Bern
SWITZERLAND Tel:(+41) 31 631 23 78
Fax: (+41) 31 631 25 34

The detailed rules of the Pet Transport Scheme have been put on the Internet and will be sent to enquirers on request.

The countries and territories from which animals may come under PETS are:

- Andorra
- Austria
- Belgium
- Denmark
- Finland
- France
- Germany
- Gibraltar
- Greece
- Iceland
- Italy
- Liechtenstein
- Luxembourg
- Monaco
- The Netherlands
- Norway
- Portugal
- San Marino
- Spain
- Sweden
- Switzerland
- Vatican City

At the time of writing, the pilot scheme relates to the UK only. An announcement by the Irish authorities concerning the arrangements for pet cats and dogs entering the Republic of Ireland against the backdrop of the PETS project in the UK is expected to be made at any time.

The expert Group set up by the Government to look at the question of modernising the quarantine regulations was chaired by Professor Ian Kennedy, of University College London. Professor Kennedy's Group reported in September 1998 recommending radical changes, and the result has been the new PETS scheme.

For readers who wish to find out the latest on the PETS scheme, a summary of the recommendations by Professor Kennedy are available on the Internet at http://maff.gov.uk/animalh/quarantine/default.htm, and copies of the full report (price £15) are available from: MAFF Publications, Admail 6000, London SW1A 2XX. Telephone: 0645 556 000

Details are also available from the MAFF website at http://maff.gov.uk/animalh/quarantine/movement/movement.htm, or the Pet Travel Scheme Helpline on 020 8330 6835 (fax: 020 8330 8304), or email the Helpline at pets@ahvg.maff.gov.uk.

CODE OF CONDUCT FOR KEEPERS AND BREEDERS OF JACK RUSSELL TERRIERS

It is incumbent on every owner of a Jack Russell terrier to do everything in their power to ensure that the breed continues to go from strength to strength, and that nothing happens which can be used by our opponents. There are people, individuals and organisations, who would rather that we did not keep, work and/or show our terriers. True, they are in a minority, but a very vociferous and vocal minority, who tend to get publicity and the ears of politicians to a degree far out of proportion to their numbers. These are the people who will latch on to anything that we, or our terriers, do (or don't do, in some cases), and use this as ammunition with which to shoot us down. It is vital, therefore, that we all adhere to a strict code of conduct at all times. Remember, the first time you do something wrong is the time that you will be noticed, and your actions my result in a lot of trouble for yourself, your terrier(s) and even other JR owners.

With this in mind, I write this Code of Conduct which, to me, seems to be based on nothing other than common sense. It is in no way legally enforceable, nor does it seek to undermine, replace or circumvent other codes put in place by clubs or societies. Rather, this code is intended to complement any other codes which exist, and I hope that all readers will bear this in mind at all times.

The main theme of my code is simple – 'Think!'

1. All Jack Russell terriers must be correctly fed, housed, watered, exercised and generally cared for at all times
2. When appropriate, veterinary care must be sought for any or all JRs under your care.
3. No JR should be left as a 'latch key' dog, i.e. you must not allow your JR to roam at large.
4. Do not allow your JR, or your activities linked with the keeping of your JR, to become a nuisance to neighbours. Not everyone likes dogs.
5. At all times, other than when working, all JRs should wear a collar with

Tinker, or 'Mr T' to his friends, was twelve years old when this photograph was taken. At the time of writing he is seventeen and still enjoys a good sniff around the fields and hedgerows of Wiltshire.

an approved identity tag attached. This tag should carry the name and telephone number(s) of the owner(s) and the veterinary surgeon.

6. All JRs should be under proper control at all times and, when walking alongside a highway, the JR should be on a leash of appropriate length and strength.

7. Owners and exercisers of JRs should always remove all faeces produced by their dog(s), and dispose of it in an appropriate manner.

8. Where it is proved or suspected that a dog or a bitch is carrying any deleterious genes, the animal(s) in question will not be used for any breeding purpose.

9. No JR of poor or questionable temperament will be used for breeding purposes of any kind.

10. All efforts must be made to ensure that new purchasers of JRs are made aware of what they are taking on, and can provide the dog(s) with the appropriate home and care.

11. A JR's characteristics and/or 'pedigree' shall not knowingly be misrepresented to any prospective buyer.

12. When selling a JR, the owner shall pass on to the new owner all relevant paperwork, pedigrees, registration documents, vaccination records, etc. In the case of a puppy, the breeder shall also give to the new owner full details of the puppy's diet.

INDEX